Prevenient Grace

God's Gift of Spiritual Breadcrumbs

Shirley J Foor

FLOATING LEAF PRESS

CHARLOTTE, NORTH CAROLINA

Copyright © 2020 by Shirley J Foor. All rights reserved. With the exception of short quotations for articles and reviews, no part of this publication may be reproduced, transmitted, scanned, distributed, stored in any form or by any means, electronic, mechanical, photocopying, recording, or otherwise, without prior written permission from the author.

Cover photo by Shirley J Foor

Published in the United States of America by

FLOATING LEAF PRESS

A division of
WordPlay

Maureen Ryan Griffin

6420 A-1 Rea Road, Suite 218, Charlotte, NC 28277

Phone: 704-494-9961

Email: info@wordplaynow.com

www.wordplaynow.com

ISBN 978-1-950499-13-7

To the *still small voice*
that commissioned my words
to His purpose,
and to my spiritual mentors,
Kathy and Natalie,
who read my stories to ensure
my truth to the purpose

Contents

"Prevenient Grace" Comes to Light 7
An Introduction to Prevenient Grace 9

Story of Faithfulness 19

The Devil and the Blue Bench 20
Learning at the Seat of Contempt 31
Racing Down Deadman's Hill 38
Time for a Revival 43

Repentance 53

Practice, Practice, Practice 54
Stories of Family Prevenient Grace 63
Them Bones, Them Bones 64

Thanksgiving for Deliverance 68

Please, Please, Not My Beautiful Little Girl 69
The Little Old Lady in Sneakers 73
An Abrupt Turn of Events 77
The Mentor Most Mysterious 88

Words of Absolute Praise 101

God has a sense of humor.. 102
I Need a Jeep 103
I Forgot to Check the Thyme 109

God's Creativity 118

Drive Through It! Drive Through It!........................... 119

Glory to God at Cracker Barrel 125

Success after 57 Years 126
25 Time and Tide and All that Jazz 133

Refuge in the Light 141

Epilogue 142
About the Author 147
Confound It!: A Collection of Recollections 149

"Prevenient Grace" Comes to Light

"Wait! You want me to do what, God?"

"I want you to write about the pictures that I have shown to you."

"But those are personal pictures, God. Personal stories. Who cares a whit about what I experienced? I'm a nobody. They will think I am full of myself to write about these things, much less publish them in a book."

"Do you think I care about what 'they' think, child? I already know about 'they.'"

"Yes, I know that, but for me to tell someone that 'God told me to write this book about prevenient grace' leaves me way out there among my family and friends."

"Do you remember the words with the pictures I showed to you?"

"Yes, God. I heard a voice in my brain telling me 'I was with you,' and 'I was there.'"

"Well, I am with you now. I have selected you for this task because I know that it is within your power to do it, as only you can. I was with you in all of those times in your past; I am with you now."

Sigh. So, here I am. To be clear, I did not hear an audible voice. But those "God" thoughts crowded my thoughts out of the way and took their own undeniable form. You'll understand in your days ahead as you meet your gifts of prevenient grace.

Regardless of what you might think about this project, this book began with that dialogue. In the middle of the night, in the darkness of many nights in 2019. With the words in my brain, a series of vignettes, all scenes from my life, and the ethereal phrases "I was with you," or "I was there" attached. The scenes appeared as I was falling asleep, or driving somewhere, or sitting with an iced tea in my hand, watching the hummingbirds feed at the firebush. Anytime, anyplace. It was spooky. Later, as I revisited those scenes in my writing, still other scenes of past experiences appeared. I have included some of the stories prompted by those pictures, as well.

If you are not, or have not, been given to conversing with God, be prepared. This book might well open your heart to the experience. Although your experiences will differ from mine, you have had them.

PREVENIENT GRACE

You might have considered them "lucky" experiences. You might even have uttered, as I have, phrases such as, "There, but for the grace of God . . .," or "Man, I was lucky that time." Man had nothing to do with any of it.

This book is not a philosophical treatise on what the premise of prevenient grace means in one's life. Prevenient grace is personal. Very personal. You cannot devise a system to explain prevenient grace as you might solve a mathematical equation or knit a sweater from a pattern. Prevenient grace is the clear expression of God's hand in your life. Once you gain an understanding of how the invisible prevenient grace become visible, the images gathered from your life will appear again and again. Those images from the past are gifts of grace that preview the gifts that will come naturally in your walk with God.

I believe that this book is intended to help you recognize and appreciate the times when God was determined to lead you to Him. The events in your recollections will be significant, significant enough to act as the mental two-by-four moment of awareness of God's plan for you. Most certainly, some of us take longer than others to embrace the recognition and the awareness. The length of time is irrelevant. What counts most is that we finally do recognize and embrace the jolt of understanding in the moment.

Let your discovery begin. You can be sure, too, that His gifts of grace do not end with your discovery.

SJF

An Introduction to Prevenient Grace

Prevenient grace.

    Hardly a familiar phrase, but it is a significant one. It would be my guess, however, that only a cathedral-size group of Christians, among all of Christians, knows the term "prevenient grace" or its meaning. Many of those whom I call the "professional" Christians, the ones who can quote scripture without turning a page in their Bible, have no knowledge of "prevenient grace."
    I first heard that phrase on my three-day Walk to Emmaus, a program of spiritual discovery, under the auspices of The Upper Room, a devotion and ministry organization associated with the Methodist Church. The Walk to Emmaus program is a modern-day expression of the events that occurred during the three days that followed Christ's resurrection.

To be honest, I failed to grasp the significance of prevenient grace when I participated in the program. The speaker did not seem to have a clear understanding of the topic. Or, perhaps, she was unable to communicate what she knew. In either case, my understanding of prevenient grace was cloudy, at best. The collection of circumstances was not kind to the presenter or to me.

I believe that a couple of explanations are necessary so that you have a better understanding of both The Walk to Emmaus and the idea of "prevenient grace." According to The Upper Room website, The Walk to Emmaus offers believers ". . . the opportunity to rediscover Christ's presence in their lives, to gain a fresh understanding of God's transforming grace, and to form friendships that foster and support spiritual maturity." We "pilgrims," as we were called, experienced an intense immersion in scripture-based, New-Testament thinking, including prevenient grace. The Walk to Emmaus is important only because that is where I gained the thread of understanding and the change of heart that is the foundation for this book.

Prevenient grace, as described by Thomas Oden, a Methodist theologian and author who influenced the development of Methodism in England and in the United States, is "the grace that draws persons closer to

God, lessens their blindness to divine remedies, strengthens their will to accept revealed truth, and enables repentance."

In general, scholars say the gift of prevenient grace comes in two premises: the irresistible gift and the resistible gift. Thomas Oden describes these competing viewpoints in this way: the first—irresistible grace—is promoted by the Calvinists, the followers of John Calvin. Calvin believed that God selects certain persons to whom He grants prevenient grace.

Because Calvin believed that one's life is predestined, those who receive the gift of grace will forever hold it dear. Jacob Arminius, a prominent Dutch theologian, took exception to the notion of predestination. He believed that the gift of prevenient grace is given to all and is resistible because free will is a gift from Christ's sacrifice on the cross and for their journey with Christ.

Now that the explanations are out of the way, let's get on with the "why" of this book of prevenient grace stories.

In the days after the Walk to Emmaus experience, I traveled through my world as a different person. I looked the same, but I was at peace with myself and my world, as never before. There had been no clap of thunder or bolt of lightning to signal a transformation.

No rending of garments. No shouting. Nothing dramatic. God had worked quietly to gain my full attention after all the years of coaxing me.

Soon thereafter, this prevenient-grace thing began to manifest its history with me. A series of mental vignettes – specific, vivid scenes that seemed to be rising from the mist of my past. Kind of like the old-fashioned portrait photos that fade into the background without a border. With each scene, I heard the words "I was with you," or "I was there." The specifics of those vignettes, which replayed vividly in my mind, will come later.

From my perspective, these times of prevenient grace are like God dropping spiritual breadcrumbs in our lives. With each spiritual crumb, He gives the nonbeliever glimpses of His grace, until the nonbeliever is ready to recognize and to accept His redeeming word. In my early years, I believed in God, but I was not yet walking in concert with God. Just from being in the world, I believed that He existed, primarily from the spending time with friends and acquaintances. Yet, in my mind, He lived in this ethereal place called heaven, somewhere beyond the clouds.

My church-going friends repeatedly praised Him for one thing or another. They praised Him out of the blue, like they were greeting a friend. I was aware of the entity called "God" and that He had a son, Jesus, who died on the cross for all of us sinners.

Furthermore, I had often thanked "Him" and asked "Him" to take some ugliness from me or from someone in my family. Why? Because it seemed like the thing to do. Even though I was not one with Him, He was right there next to me. He had touched my life many times and in many ways through the spiritual breadcrumbs.

Though I was aware that I had somehow avoided a heap of pain and ugliness, even death, I did not understand that these events were gifts of divine grace.

Nor could I embrace the truth of what I had experienced because I lacked understanding. Like many Christians, the gift of prevenient grace escaped my knowledge and appreciation.

The thing about prevenient grace is that, when we don't know about it, we give the spiritual breadcrumbs other words and meanings. When the grace involves good fortune or a warning, we might think, "Boy, was I lucky!" or "How did that happen?" The spiritual crumbs take such diverse forms of messaging that if we are not paying attention, we will miss the point, oblivious to the importance of the "coincidental" events. It takes some of us longer than others to pay attention. It took me 70+ years.

God started dropping crumbs when I was seven, and He has consistently, determinedly dropped them in the years since. When I was 12, I enjoyed a full day of prevenient grace in a couple of ways. Later, He dropped them when my beautiful daughter was afflicted with an ugly, disfiguring disease. Oh, and then there's the time . . . The stories from over the 70 years are abundant.

When I finally noticed the crumbs after my Walk to Emmaus experience a couple of years ago, my life has not been the same. Actually, I did not notice, but The Walk, another moment of prevenient grace, opened my mind to what God wanted me to know. So, He showed me the vignettes, the softened scenes to remind me that "I was with you."

The moments of grace that I have experienced are what I share in these stories, fuller versions of the vignettes. I suspect that you may pooh-pooh the stories because I "couldn't possibly" recall them as I do. Well, let me say this about that: The facts (the who, what, where, when, why, and how) of each story are true. The rest of each story is an expression of the events to the best of my recollection.

Why should you, the reader, bother to trouble yourself to consider, much less give credence to, my words? Well, I can think of no specific reason that you should. I am no one of note. I am no better or wiser than you. I have no impressive credentials that might elevate my status.

On the other hand, I just might be a moment of prevenient grace in your journey. What you read may well prompt you to visit some of the spiritual crumbs—prevenient grace—in your earlier days. Just saying. It is possible that once you open the door to your awareness of prevenient grace, the wind of grace will chase the dust bunnies of your unbelief, or maybe give renewed joy to your belief.

I pray that you see the work of His prevenient grace in your life.

Story of Faithfulness

As you saved David,
You have saved me countless times.
I was unaware.

You share images
Of times when your grace held me.
I hear, "I was there."

Scenes of childhood folly
Play in my mind, and I hear,
"I was with you then."

With these scenes of favor
I erupt in grateful joy
And pure thanksgiving.

Your grace saved David.
That I count as David did,
Drives me to serve you.

The Devil and the Blue Bench

This moment of prevenient grace came to me as a vignette of a blue, wooden bench over a creek near a railroad track. The water, muddied and roiled by the early snow melt, churned in the small creek. This is the "spiritual crumb" story behind the vignette. With the picture came the words, "I was with you."

I am walking home from school. My name is Shirley. I am seven years old and in the second grade at Novi Elementary School. Every day, I walk down Novi Road past the Wendland's house, the Goldsworthy's house and the lodge hall. On the corner of Novi Road and Grand River (U.S. 16 between Detroit and Lansing), one of the five corners that come together at that intersection, sits Matt Moren's general store. I like to go in there because it is full of neat stuff like thread and buttons and work shirts and pants and wheels of the "stinky foot" cheese (aged cheddar) that Grandpa Kent likes. Not today, though.

Mr. Martin, Grandma Kent's next door neighbor, sits on a bench on the porch at the store. He waves.

"Hello, Shirley. On your way home?" He hollers. I am a little distance away, close to the roadway.

"Yes, sir." I holler back.

"You be careful. Pay attention. You hear?"

"Yes, sir." Mr. Martin sits there nearly every day, and he always says the same thing. He's old. "Thank you, Mr. Martin." We wave.

The next part of my walk requires that I pay extra attention. Mr. Martin knows that, and he watches me carefully. I must cross Grand River, a four-lane highway, at the five corners. This where the little Eleven Mile Road joins the intersection of the big Novi Road and bigger Grand River. I have crossed Grand River many times, but always down by the stores, at the end of Eleven Mile Road, where Grandma lives up on hill. She sends me to Harnden's Grocery Store for bread and lettuce, sometimes canned goods, stuff like that. When I cross there, I just have to look both ways for cars. There usually aren't many.

When I cross at the corners, though, I have to watch for the green light across from me and for any traffic that might be turning from one of the other corners. After that, I have to watch for cars that might turn into the Mobil station next to me. After I pass the gas station, the rest of my trip is just about walking.

Mrs. Ballard waves from her front porch, next to the Baptist church. She is there nearly every day, as I start up the hill to the old cemetery. My mother's grandparents—Woodruff and Kent—are buried there. I hop across the cracks in the sidewalk on my way up to the cemetery.

I went into the cemetery one day. The black iron gate was open. I just walked around and looked at the big stone things (Grandma told me they are called "head stones" because they sit at the head of the dead person.) with letters and numbers on them. I could read the numbers and the letters, but I didn't understand what they meant. Most of the numbers and letters were covered in yucky green stuff, anyway. The gate is open again today, but I am not stopping. Today, I am to, "Just walk straight home!" That's what my Mother and Grandma said to do.

I start hopping over cracks in the sidewalk again. Hopping is easier when I'm not wearing my clunky rubber boots. Mom said I could go without boots today because the snow is mostly gone, and the weather is nice. I hop, and I hop. I hopped up hill to the cemetery. Now I am hopping downhill toward the railroad tracks.

Hopping is harder going downhill. I really have to pay attention.

On my last hop, I lose my balance. I stumble a little, then begin to hop again.

"That's really weird." As I started to hop, I see a blue bench over the creek next to the railroad tracks. "Who would put a bench there?" I wondered. "That's dumb. Nobody can sit on it. They would get their feet wet in the creek." I continued to wonder. "If someone needs to cross the creek, they could just go down to the railroad tracks. Besides that, there is nothing but weeds and thistle on the other side. Really dumb." But the "dumb idea" had my attention.

I walked to the edge of the creek and considered the bench for a minute. "I'll bet I can cross the creek." I looked at the water speeding along under the bench. Muddy and kind of scary. "Yeah. I can do it. I'll just have to be slow and careful."

I wiggled the bench to see how steady it is. "Feels okay," I think. I grab the sides of the bench and bring one leg up onto it. I wait to see how it feels, then slowly pull my other leg up. I watch the water and hear it talking to itself.

I scoot slowly and move carefully. My fat snowsuit legs get in the way. I stop and start again. I had crawled about halfway across when my right leg slipped off the bench into the water. I don't know why I slipped. I hadn't wobbled or anything." That leg slipped into the water, and the rest of me followed. I managed to hold onto the bench. "Oh, man. Mother is going to be so mad that I got my school shoes wet. And my snowsuit. I am going to be in such trouble." I struggled a little to hold on to the bench. I had broken all the rules. Mother's rules. Grandma's rules. I didn't "come straight home!"

The water is pushing hard against me. Bumping me around. Making my fingers tired, trying to hold on. My snowsuit is getting heavy. I have to figure a way out of this.

•. •. •. •. •

Now, I am across the tracks on Novi Road, walking against the traffic like I always do, but I am running and walking, running and walking. I don't want to be later than I am. Mother is going to be worried and angry because I am late getting home. "What am I going to tell my mother about this?" I wonder, glancing down at my wet snowsuit and shoes as I hurry.

I stop and stand still. "Wait. What's going on?" I stop my run/walk routine in front of Morrison's house, about halfway between the railroad tracks and home.

My shoes are dry. And my snow pants. I turn to look back at the bench, but a train is crossing the roadway, so I can't see where the bench was or the creek.

"How did I get out of the creek?" I remember the creek pushing me into the bench. I remember my fingers being tired hanging onto the bench. I don't remember how I got out of the creek. I checked my shoes and snow pants again. "Yeah, they're really dry." I couldn't remember anyone stopping to help me. Mrs. Dunne drove by when I was on the hill. She waved, but she didn't stop. I was confused. I start my walk/run again, slowly, uncertain.

I am breathing hard when I come through the back door. Everything was ordinary, just like every other day. Mother hardly notices that I am home. She's busy with my little brother, Dennis. She's always busy with my brother. He's four and needs lots of help. I called, "Hi, I'm home" to her as I went to my bedroom to change into my play clothes. She never knew what had happened at the creek, and I never told her about any of it. No reason to tell her. Without wet shoes and snowsuit, I had nothing to say. I just remembered the pictures in my brain.

•.   •.   •.   •   •

The look of disbelief is stark upon your face. If I were in your shoes, I, too, would, most likely, be in a state of disbelief, and I was there for this event. Let me give you some thoughts to explain your many "Seriously?" responses.

First, you wonder why would a seven-year-old be walking home from school. Good question. World War II had recently ended, and the country was seeking some normalcy. After years of the rationing of gas, rubber, sugar, shoes, and a host of other things, normal for my family was that we had only one car. Most families were like that in those days. A car for every adult in the family was an extravagance few families could manage. My father worked as many hours as possible at the Pontiac motor car factory, 40 miles away in Pontiac, MI to ensure that his family would thrive in the post-war environment. A second car was out of the question.

My father worked second-shift, afternoons, which meant that someone could drive me to school, but I had no transportation home at 3:30 p.m. The school district did not yet provide bus service.

Additionally, in the days of the 1940s, children learned self-reliance, awareness of surroundings, and perseverance. We went everywhere on our own. Adults did not hover around us to "protect" us. AAA-sponsored Safety Patrol Girls and Safety Patrol Boys from the eighth grade were our crossing guards. They wore the Buster Brown white belts across their chests to signify their responsibility. They didn't have whistles or big STOP signs. I wanted to be a Safety Patrol Girl when I was an eighth grader. And I was.

Also, Grandma Kent had told me, in her no-nonsense voice, about not accepting rides from strangers and what to do if someone offered me treats to help them find their "lost puppy," or some other lame story. I was not fearful because she had taught me about the important things. I didn't need to be frightened when I was alone in the world, but she said I did need to pay attention, and be careful. Therefore, walking home from school, even for a seven-year-old, was no big deal.

What about the bench over the creek? Yes, there is the business of the useless, but inviting, blue bench. How did the bench get there? Who put it there? To what end? My questions were many. I didn't have an explanation for any of the picture I remembered at the time, but I think I do now. I believe that the devil (yes, the devil, the evil one) put the bench there to tantalize a curious, daring seven-year-old. He hooked me. I believe I am right because when Mother drove me to school the next morning, the bench was gone. Not a single blue board lay anywhere in the weedy flat next to the creek.

Okay. So, the devil put the bench there. How did a little kid manage to hold onto it with her tiny hands against the weight of her wet snowsuit and the rush of the water? Another good question. Perhaps that was my first moment of prevenient grace. I knew God's name, but I had no idea what God did. I also knew of the word "miracle," but miracle was just a word for adults to use. Now, however, I believe the word "miracle" applies in this situation. God took away the devil's joy.

If so, then, why would I worry what my mother thought about my ruined shoes and wet snowsuit, rather than dying in the swollen creek? You certainly are good at asking questions.

Death had not yet touched my life. All of my relatives, including both sets of my grandparents and one great grandmother, were still alive. I had not experienced death in any personal way. Not even the death of a pet.

Death was only a word. Mother would kill one of our orange gold Buff Orpington hens for Sunday dinner, but that death had nothing to do with me. Uncle Homer would cart one of our white-faced steers off to the packing house, and a few days later he would come home with a pile of white packages of hamburger, steaks and roasts. The death of our "cow" had nothing to do with me. My grandfather paid me a nickel for every tomato worm that I squished under a rock or under my foot to protect our tomato crop. Those wormy deaths had nothing to do with me, either. So, death, too, was just a word.

Now for your big question: How could I possibly remember something from so long ago? Isn't it possible that I am given to drama? Anything is possible. Nevertheless, considering that the appearance of the vignette dropped me into an aged video, with the words "I was with you," I am compelled to believe the story resulted from a gift of prevenient grace for my future.

I cannot remember when I had last thought of this trip home from school, but the vignette brought it back to let me hear it and see it. I didn't have to think about the story; I lived it again. Kids don't dwell on stories like this. We are too busy growing up, doing things like riding bikes and climbing trees and stuff like that. Generally speaking, kids live in the "that was then, this is now" kind of existence.

Still, the vignette and the "I was with you" brought back the smell and sound of the creek and the day, the fear of my mother's wrath, and the feeling of the creek pushing me. It also brought back the puzzling explanation of how I managed to get out of the water and back onto the roadway.

The Lord had gifted me with continued life. Perhaps God had this day, the writing of this story, all of these stories in this book, in my future. Only God knows for sure.

Learning at the Seat of Contempt

Lest you come to believe that the gifts of prevenient grace are all granted on a one-to-one basis, I can testify that they are not. God meets us where we are, and sometimes that takes a cast of many, as it did in this story. Because this was such an unlikely coming together of families, I easily attribute this clashing of standards— moral, ethical, even decency —to God effecting change through a dose of reality among the disparate clans. I suspect that you can think back to dramatic changes in groups you know or have worked with over time. The changes didn't just happen. No, you can be sure that God was in the midst of the confusion and the challenges to effect those changes. That's just what happened with our contentious family; God met us at a time when we were relaxed and not expecting to learn.

Friends invited our family to a snazzy company-sponsored retreat in the country one summer. The place had pleasant cabins tucked among acres of trees that surrounded a very big lake. The dad in the other family worked as an executive in a major business-machine corporation that rewarded its executives with vacation time at "The Farm." The company allowed executives to invite friends to the facility.

I never thought of our families—the Sinclairs and the Snows— as being friends. I was in the same grade as their daughter, Donna, and our moms volunteered in the community and belonged to a couple of the same social groups. But my dad was a factory worker, not a neat-and-tidy executive like Mr. Sinclair. When my dad came home, his clothes were dirty and, often, his hands were cut up and ugly from a miscue at the lathe he used to trim the pieces of metal that he shaped. Once in a while, the adults in several local families, including mine, would get together to play pinochle, but that was pretty much it.

Basically, the only thing the families had in common was us kids—three girls, three boys collectively.

The deal for this vacation was that my family would stay in a cabin separate from theirs, but we would share potluck evening meals on their screened porch.

This story is important to me because the event changed the lives in my household. For sure, that week drastically changed the behaviors of my two brothers and me. We were transformed from constant adversaries who squabbled about anything and over anything into decent siblings. Compared to the cruel children we spent that week with, my brothers and I would qualify as angels.

We arrived at The Farm on Sunday evening, which was spent exploring our cabin and its surroundings. Then, while the adults talked, we girls investigated the possibilities for the next day. For openers, we made plans to go rowing in the morning. Our rowing exceeded the morning, however. Donna, Christy, and I spent hours rowing and hiking around this enormous, interesting lake. We talked and talked and laughed and kept rowing and hiking. I had no idea what the boys were doing. Didn't much care, either.

The impetus for our post-vacation transformation began to take shape during the times our families were together. As a rule, my brothers and I argued and fussed and fumed and drove our parents to distractions, as adults are given to saying. As combative as we were at home, nothing we had done even came close to the shock of the family time experience with the Sinclairs. Their family was the epitome of "all is not as it seems."

Mr. and Mrs. Sinclair were both super involved in their Baptist church. The rules of their church were very important to them. "Upstanding members" of the church was how they were talked about in the community. As a 12-year-old kid, I thought their church participation was more of a mystery. For instance, although I never saw evidence of this myself, their "love of the drink" was well known throughout the community. I also thought they were just kind of stuffy, maybe even uppity to tell the truth.

The church stuff never spilled over into my relationship with the girls. Donna and I played jacks in the winter and roller skated around and around the school during the spring. Their younger girl, Christy, was a friend, too. We never did anything special, but, from time to time, we had fun together. The boy, Ricky, was much younger and a real pain, a smart mouth who had to be in the middle of everything, even if the conversation or event had nothing to do with him. And, like my brothers, Ricky could do no wrong.

Anyway, we all gathered at the Sinclair's cabin for our casual potluck supper Sunday on the screened porch. Nothing fancy. Hamburgers, hot dogs, potato salad, chips. All the important stuff. Then it started.

"Ricky, bring the napkins from the kitchen." Mrs. S. said. No "please" attached. Ricky was maybe nine years old.

Ricky: "You do it. I'm hungry, and I'm not your slave."

What's wrong with this picture? Ricky's being disrespectful to his mother and Mr. S. isn't correcting him? Mrs. S. went for the napkins.

Mr. S.: "Dana, would you get the ketchup? Your mother forgot it." Huh? It doesn't matter who forgot the ketchup, but Mr. S. had to lay blame on Mrs. S. Furthermore, he was not about to get the ketchup himself. He was too cool to move.

Dana: "How can anyone be so stupid? She should get it. She forgot it." Why did Mrs. S. put up with comments like those? And how does any kid get away with speaking about a parent that way?

What is this? Beat up on Mrs. S. night? Not to put too fine a point on this, but the kids were rude and obnoxious to their mother throughout the rest of the meal. Besides that, Mr. S. did nothing in defense of his wife or to curtail his children's rudeness. My brothers and I sat dumbfounded. Man, if any of the three of us had ever spoken to our mom like that, Dad would have taken the offending child outside for a good "talking to."

We looked to our parents for direction. What we got was the stern but cool "keep your mouth shut" look. Mom didn't interrupt her conversation, but we knew the message behind "that" look, so we kept eating.

I would like to say that this experience in abusive behavior was a one-time thing, but it sure as the dickens was not. The Snow family shared two more joint meals with the Sinclairs. Each was prickly with disrespect from the children and disinterest from Mr. S. It was like he couldn't be bothered with anyone or anything, unless it pertained to him. Somehow, our potlucks ended, and we Snows ate on our own screened porch. We ate quietly. None of us said a word about anything we had seen and heard on the other porch. Those evenings had been way too unbelievable to think about, much less speak about out loud, in real words.

The result of our experience was this: My brothers and I might occasionally get snarky in a touchy moment, but the week with the Sinclairs was so stunning in its offensiveness that our being nice to one another became routine, and the responding "please" and "thank you" were nearly overdone.

To this day, more than 60 years later, the words and the pictures of the exchanges between those children and their mother are just as vivid and as disgusting as in the days I lived through them. Just as clear and reprehensible, too, is the image of Mr. S., sitting so prim and proper, smug and aloof as his bratty, spoiled children disrespected his wife of many years.

PREVENIENT GRACE

The girls and I continued to get along in school. We weren't quite so chummy as we once were, but we did get along. Moreover, I surely didn't think so much of Mr. S. He was an adult not to be trusted. Even if he was a big deal in his church.

My brothers and I had experienced the emotional equivalent of shock therapy. We stopped being unruly heathens. We still got into the occasional squabble, but we did not engage in our previous bickering and picking at one another. We also noticed that, for all our unruly behavior, we respected our parents and would never had thought to speak to or treat our mother as the Sinclair children had treated theirs. Unlike Mr. Sinclair, our father would not have let us get away with sassiness and disrespect like that. His dislike would not have ended well for us.

Racing Down Deadman's Hill

We fearless sled riders never called it Deadman's Hill, but after one afternoon of crazy sledding on that hill, I thought it easily could become that name.

For most of the winter, six or eight of us grade schoolers, between the ages of eight and 12, would drag our Flexible Flyer sleds down 11-Mile Road, past my Grandmother Kent's house to Putnam's Hill. The basic group of sled riders—Ricky, Billy, Allen, Clifford and me—met at the bottom of my grandmother's driveway on the hill. Other riders came and went, depending on the weather. From Grandma Kent's house, we talked little and hurried along toward the hill, about a half mile away, to take advantage of as much daylight as possible.

We stepped on the flattened, rusted wire fence, and carried or bumped our sleds over the fence behind us, and marched a few yards to the top of the hill. This hill had a long, wide slope toward Grand River, the main highway between Detroit and Lansing. Big, tall trees dotted the landscape on either side of the slope.

One winter, our ordinary playfulness changed from individual head-to-head races and competitive downhill heats to something more sinister. Sometimes we were too inventive for our own good. Maybe it had something to do with our getting older, but not wiser. This became one of those times.

Generally, we made great sport of starting with two or three racers (depending upon the number of participants we had) at the top of the hill. We raucously launched the race with a loud, "GO!" The racers, hands on sleds, ran along side of their Flyers and flopped aboard when they felt ready. Racers took turns standing watch at the bottom of the hill to determine the winner of the heat. We competed in a spirit of friendship, not rules. Sure, we had our squabbles, but we wanted to race our sleds, so we quickly settled that nonsense. The speed was exhilarating, excitement ran high.

We stayed on the hill until the sun dropped behind the trees and sent long shadows over our raceway. The length of the shadows was the signal that our moms would be expecting us home for supper, very soon.

Over our hours of daily racing, the hill gained an icy sheen, and the races grew faster. The speed was thrilling!

Nevertheless, Ricky, the daredevil in our group (there always is one), wanted to do more. He thought it would be fun to make a line of sleds and weave among the tall, dark trees that had witnessed our many races. Sounded like a good idea at the time.

I was the lead sled in the first downhill run. I hooked my black-booted toes into the steering loop of the sled behind me. Each sled rider did the same, until all sleds—six of us—were connected. Then we pushed off.

Together, we sort of paddled our way down the hill to gain some momentum. Within seconds, our line of sleds was weaving downhill among the sturdy trees, through fresh, soft, white snow, which kept our early trips under control. As the lead sled, I kept the line of travel fairly straight through the trees the first time through. I was not a fan of crack-the-whip games.

We laughed and shouted with the speed, the wind, and the excitement of racing among the towering trees. When we slowed to a stop at the bottom of the hill, the motorists on Grand River, who had watched our trip downhill as they waited at the traffic light, honked and waved from rolled-down windows. We waved back and turned to trudge up the hill for another run. We were never close to the highway when we ended our downhill runs.

PREVENIENT GRACE

After the second run, I dropped back to the last-sled position. Something had been bothering me about this game since the first run, and I wanted a fresh perspective. (No one would have suspected me of being a mother hen, but I was.) As we zoomed down the hill on the third run, I realized that we were playing a really deadly version of crack-the-whip. Six loaded sleds whipping around the trees, gaining speed, young riders engaged in careless fun. The ride was scary in its possibilities.

Weaving around the huge trees at an ever-increasing speed was treacherous folly. The last two or three sled riders were in danger. If the leader of the pack became too daring, or riders weren't paying attention, the end of the whip could slam into a tree and the rider be seriously hurt. Or worse.

I was the eldest of the lot, which isn't saying a much. I was 12 years old, a responsible 12-year-old. My grandmother, whom I always stopped to see on my way to the hill, reminded me that when I was the eldest of the bunch, I needed to pay attention to the little ones in the group. Be sure they were up to what we older ones planned to do. "Little ones are not fast thinkers. You need to think for them." She told me. "Yes, Gramma," She knew I would.

After the second run, those little ones were top on my mind. "Hey, guys. What do say we run two whips? One on this side of the hill and another over there, on the other side of the hill. That way, everybody can have a turn at leading."

Clifford, one of the younger boys, said, "Yeah! Let's do that!" Later, he said, quietly, that the last time we went down in the long line, it really scared him.

"Me, too." I thought. Man, I truly didn't want an accident to turn our winter playground into Deadman's Hill. If any of us had gotten hurt, even a little bit, the adults would never let us come back. Then what would we do?

That I had become the voice of reason here was suspicious, at best. There was more at work here than my grandmother's admonition about watching over the little kids. When it came to having fun on the hill and going faster and trying new things, I usually was the leader of the pack. Whipping around the trees in a line of sleds was my kind of fun. The gift of prevenient grace probably saved us from bodily harm. Funny thing about all that changing of practices, it seemed like the right thing to do. Huh. Imagine that.

Time for a Revival

With this vignette, I saw a huge, well-worn tent sitting in a field. The tent had a black-and-white sign across its front that announced the purpose for the tent. "I was there with you all night." I know now that He certainly was.

What is a "revival meeting"? I wondered, as I walked across the carnival grounds.

The monster brown tent in the far corner had a huge sign with thick black letters: REVIVAL MEETING TONIGHT. I saw the sign, then I saw Mrs. Hicks talking with some men in front of the tent opening. She looked like she was excited about something. If Mrs. Hicks was excited, standing in front of that tent, chances are the "revival meeting" has something to do with religion. The only thing missing was Mrs. Hicks's black Bible, which she usually clutched to her chest. If she and her Bible showed up at the revival tent tonight, then the "revival" surely was a religious meeting of some kind.

I had spent the day at the carnival, trying some of the rides, which I didn't like, and won the bicycle race in the afternoon. I liked that for sure. I had beaten seven boys for the prize of a week's worth of Mrs. Gaffney's super delicious burgers. As good as that part of the carnival had been, my innate curiosity drew me to the possibility of slipping into the Revival Meeting.

It would be fairly easy to come back. I was staying at my Grandma Kent's house, just three blocks away, for the weekend. The carnival was there all weekend. (My family was, I believe, eager for me to be gone. They certainly did not attend any part of the carnival. Not even the bicycle race that I won.) I just needed Gram's permission.

After dinner, I asked "Gram? Would it be okay if I went back to the carnival with Emily and Grace tonight?" We girls had talked about getting together, but we hadn't made any firm plans. If they came, they came. If not, well, they didn't. No matter. Going to that revival meeting was my goal.

"Why do you want to go back?" Grandma asked.

"Because we want to see what it's like at night. Things are different at night." We also lived in a small country town, about 500 residents, and the carnival was the biggest thing we had seen, ever. The carnival had set up in a huge lot on the major highway, which made it convenient for folks from several larger communities that also were short on entertainment to "come to town."

"It's that 'difference' I am concerned about." She said as she gave me her stern "Grandma look."

"We will be okay, Gram." I replied. "You know we won't do anything we shouldn't." This time, she looked at me with her stern "Shirley Jean" look. She knew that Emily and Grace were "good" girls. My behavior, on the other hand, was "iffy," given my keen curiosity. "Chief Begoll and his guys are everywhere. He probably will have more of his guys working tonight. And they know us." Because Novi was such a small place, if you have lived in town for more than six weeks, then people knew you. If not by name, then as a "familiar" stranger.

Gram smiled and shooed me out of the house. I was back at the carnival by about 7 p.m. My friends and I had agreed to meet at the cotton-candy booth. If they came back, that is. So, I headed there. The revival tent was away from the bustle of the crowd, which made it more mysterious looking. And strangely inviting. A couple of men from the tent were passing out leaflets about the "meeting." I accepted one of the papers because I wanted to know as much as I could. I was disappointed in the information on the leaflet. I guess Revival Meeting meant something to the adults.

Emily and Grace did show up. Just as I had hoped, their interest faded quickly. The night activity was too different for them. Scary for Emily. Their interest flat out died when I suggested that we could check out the revival tent. They left; I went to the Revival Meeting.

•. •. •. • •

Here's the deal about the revival-meeting thing: I both wanted to see why this meeting was so important. But where the flyer said the meeting was bound to "stir your spirit," I felt the brakes dragging. I had no idea what it meant to "stir my spirit," but for some reason the words raised the hairs on the back of my neck.

Religion was not mentioned in our house. My Dad said he wouldn't let any "damn invisible thing" tell him what to do or when to do it. Dad was the law. He was the only one in our family entitled to wants or opinions. Besides that, I didn't know enough about God to speak up. And if I had, he probably would have given me a backhand for my impertinence.

Still, I wanted to know stuff. What mysterious events happened in a Revival Meeting?

I had been searching for an experience with "religion" as long as I could remember. In my 12 years of searching, I attended the Baptist church with Mrs. Hills, my fourth-grade teacher. I attended the Methodist church with my Aunt Geraldine. I attended the Evangelical United Brethren church with friends. I had explored other churches, but none of them felt good to me.

Perhaps those church experiences didn't feel "right" because I was fearful. I was sure Dad would have pitched an ugly fit if he knew or even suspected that I was thinking of taking up with a church of any kind. Nevertheless, my need to know was bigger than the threat of a walloping with his razor strop. That's how it was between me and my curiosity.

Actually, churches made me feel uneasy. The Baptist Church has too many "can'ts." Can't dance. Can't play cards. Girls can't wear "pants," as in jeans. Seemed like the Baptists couldn't have fun. The restriction on fun put the Baptists out of the running. The Evangelical United Brethren was just the opposite: too wishy washy. That church didn't seem to have enough dos and don'ts. I guess I was kind of like Goldilocks. She was looking for just the right porridge; I was looking for just the right church.

Getting back to my dilemma. Dad was working overtime 40 miles away, and it was unlikely that he would ever see anyone who was in this tent tonight. I was betting on that probability. The only time my father left home was to play golf, and I doubted that anyone at this meeting played golf. I was betting on that, too, and the unlikely thought that any of these adults would remember me. Adults usually are so involved with themselves that they don't notice a quiet, unassuming 12-year-old kid, especially a girl child. I stayed out of the way to increase my odds of success.

I held back as the town's folk filed into the tent. This was one time I was glad the adults didn't care about or notice children. When the crowd became a scraggly flow of latecomers, I slipped around the tent flap and into the back corner, still out of the way, behind the last row of folks seated there. Other adults came in and pushed me farther back in the tent and tighter into the corner. As I said, adults are really good at ignoring kids, or pushing them around because we are just a bother.

PREVENIENT GRACE

•. •. •. • •

People kept coming in. Some were hesitant, looking around, not sure they wanted to be there. Others, like Mrs. Hicks, were just so excited and chattering energetically with others of like mind who sat in the front rows. Seats at the back of the tent were pretty tightly filled. Down front, however, many chairs awaited folks to fill them. Like my Aunt Geraldine would say when we went to church a little late, "Come late to church, and you can be sure that you will have a front-row seat." Tonight, I could see what she'd been telling me. The folks who had come early were all in the back.

The tent was dimly lighted and stuffy. It was an old tent, with conflicting scents from meetings past and many dark stories to tell, collecting still more of both tonight. It felt like the tent had a life of its own. Organ music started to play, and the crowd jostled around, settling into their seats.

Some fake-looking woman came on stage. Too much makeup. Hair too blond, too poofed up, and too stiff. She was not a welcoming person, but she was trying to be. I didn't like her attitude. She talked above the audience, in a put-on voice, like she was too good to be there with them. Too good for the poor country folks before her. We couldn't possibly know how important she was to the likes of us.

She introduced herself as Celeste. Her hand-held microphone started a piercing squeal. After the men stopped the squeal, Celeste invited us to join in singing a hymn. The words for that hymn and others were on leaflets on the chairs. Most of the people stood to sing, some did not. As tall as I was, I was a meager sapling among the imposing oaks and maples that towered above me. My voice was muffled in a veritable forest of hip pockets and jackets.

Celeste led us in another hymn, and then a man, with slicked-back hair and dressed a lot like Mr. Fisher, the man who sold used cars in a scruffy lot down by the railroad track, came onto the stage. He irritated me as much as Celeste. She was too smooth; He was too sloppy to be as smooth as he tried to be. This revival meeting was not pleasing me. I don't remember his name, but she called him Rev. Somebody. Basically, I don't remember names of people I don't like. I don't want them touching my brain.

Rev. Somebody began with a prayer. It was a long prayer. A very long prayer full of "thees" and "thous." I wondered if God needed so many words to know what the minister was trying to say. I wondered a lot of things. Things like: did the minister need to pray in that stupid, sappy, singsongy voice? Why did he have to shout? The tent was big, but not that big. Why did he look so angry as he preached? I thought God was about love, but his words were about salvation, sin, succumbing to the Holy Spirit, avoiding Satan, following God to the altar (which was just a funky stage with a speaker's table on it). I didn't understand a lot of what he shouted. I did understand that sin is bad and that most of us are really bad people. Was I that bad? The notion of being so bad bothered me.

After all of the hollering about how sinful we are, the music for "Just as I am," began to play. The hymn played on and on, verse after verse, each ending with, "Oh, lamb of God, I come, I come." Rev. Somebody pleaded with his "holy flock" to "Come forward and repent. Receive God's everlasting grace." And the people, a whole lot of them, went to the "altar."

This is where things began to get tense in my mind and my body. It was like something was pulling me toward the altar. I could feel it, but I didn't have any idea what it was. The crowd movement wasn't doing it. I avoid following crowds, especially adult crowds. Chills climbed all over me. Adults in a mass are not to be trusted. What those adults are doing is not necessarily good. Just as they ignore kids, they also will drag them into some no-good stuff. I learned when I was just a really young kid to think twice about joining adults who are milling about.

Still, I was being pulled by a strong urging to, in the reverend's words, "give myself to Christ." I didn't exactly know what that meant, but the pull was strong. Too strong. It was making me feel really spooky.

The path to the entrance had opened a bit when some of the adults between me and freedom and me going to the altar had moved forward. Why was I so skittish about this? Lots of reasons. Not the least of which was my Dad and his dislike for religion, or what he thought was religion. And if a member of his family "betrayed" his authority about religion, well, the reckoning would be ugly. For another, I had no real understanding of what I was getting myself into. The adults were way too eager, and, as I said, I didn't trust adults all that much. So, I bolted before they could take hold of me.

I literally ran the three blocks to Grandma's house. I needed to get away from the meeting before I was caught in the pull again. The carnival and the meeting tent were gone by morning, but the pull I had felt Saturday night kept chilling me. My youthful resistance exceeded that moment of prevenient grace, but the memory of the "pull" lingered. And lingers in my mind and my soul to this day.

Repentance

You were there always
Protecting me, holding me.
I did not know you.

You sent your spirit
As my life, hope slipped away.
I did not know you.

Your spirit lingered,
My heart bowed in gratefulness.
I did not know you.

Many years have passed,
My heart is again bowed low.
Yes, now I know you.

Practice, Practice, Practice

A tourist on a street in New York City stopped an older man to ask, "How do you get to Carnegie Hall?" The man looked at the tourist intently and replied, "You practice, practice, practice!" The elderly man happened to be the legendary violin virtuoso Yehudi Menuhin. He was right, of course. I have no idea whether this story is factual, but it reminded me of my introduction to the rigors of music lessons many years ago. I was not thinking about Carnegie Hall, however.

I was in eighth grade at Novi Elementary School (Michigan), and I longed to play in the band at Northville High School, where I would be enrolled in the coming fall. Actually, I didn't really know about the band. Mostly, I believed that Northville High has a band because high schools always seemed to have bands. The thought most prominent here is, all I ever truly wanted in my short life was to play music.

PREVENIENT GRACE

Early in my years, I had asked my Mother for a piano. "No!" She was emphatic. "You will lose interest, and then we'll have an expensive piece of furniture that will just take up room we don't have." She might have had a point at the time. I was in elementary school, and elementary school-age children are known for their lack of focus, long term.

Nevertheless, my little heart wanted to play music. I was so disappointed that the orange-wax, pan-pipe shaped candy whistled only one note, not many notes. I made a kazoo, but that was not satisfying, either. I wanted to play a real musical instrument. I really, really wanted to play real music. To no avail. My pleading lingered in the air like dust in the morning sunlight.

The years passed and so did the many classes of math and English and history. But no music, except, that is, for the dumb music classes. Everybody in class did the same thing, sang the same songs that sounded in the same sing-song way. Boring, boring, boring.

On Christmas break that year, I saw my friend Kathy, then a freshman at Northville High. She told me about how great it was to be in the marching band. Marching band? The high school really did have a band! (I lived in the country, many miles from the high school, and had no knowledge of what happened there.) I peppered Kathy with questions. How do you get to be in the band? What did she have to do to make that happen? She answered all of my questions. She even offered to have her dad pick me up on their way to band practice on Monday nights.

"How can I get into the band?" That was my most important question of all time.

"I didn't know that you play an instrument," she noted. Kathy played the alto saxophone. She had been taking lessons for a long time.

"I don't, but I will get one," I replied. I was so determined, so confident that I would, could accomplish my dream.

Then she spoke words of musical magic: "That's okay. They loan instruments to students. No charge." Oh, wow! If my mother thought she had dampened my musical spirit, she was wrong. So wrong.

Kathy and her dad did indeed stop for me each Monday night for the rest of the school year. I was so excited that they would take me along, that I waited on the roadside across from my house. They barely had to slow down for me to jump into the back seat of their Hudson. I was fascinated and ecstatic to watch the musicians and Mr. Lee, the director. He would tap on his music stand, and the musicians stopped playing. He talked to them about one thing or another in the music, then, he would raise his arms, baton in hand. The musicians would bring their instruments to their mouths, and he started them playing with a downbeat of his baton. I learned about downbeats and other music language on the way home from practices. I asked Kathy so many questions, and she answered them all over every mile, coming from and going to.

Along about February, as I approached graduation day, I began lobbying Mother to take me to see Mr. Lee. I explained that he was the director and would be the person to talk to about getting into the band. She resisted as relentlessly as I persisted. Finally, in April, she succumbed to my incessant nattering. I was so excited and determined that I actually called the school to see when Mr. Lee would be available. I made an appointment. That was a very bold move for this painfully shy 13-year-old. Mr. Lee agreed to meet me the day after school closed for summer break in June.

On that important day, I wore my best skirt and blouse and felt really confident. Another first for me, that confidence thing.

Mr. Lee was a kindly gentleman. He never raised his voice at band practice, even when I thought he could have, should have to the boys who clowned around. Mr. Lee stood about my height (5'8"), was sort of portly, had graying hair that receded at the temples, and was neatly dressed in a grey suit, white shirt and grey striped tie.

He greeted me cordially and seated us at a small table in his small office. I was not at all nervous, way excited, but not nervous. I was fulfilling a life-long passion.

"So, Shirley, you think you want to play in the band." He stated his question.

"Yes, sir, I do," I replied and sat up straighter.

"What instrument do you play?"

"I don't play any instrument."

He just looked at me. No expression. "How do you think you can be in the band then?" His furrowed brows turned his face into a piercing question mark.

"My friend Kathy said that the school provides instruments, and that you provide lessons."

More furrowed brows. "Do you read music?"

"No, sir, but I am sure that I can learn."

Now, raised brows.

At this point, I must say that, although I did not realize it at the time, I was one determined, if not shamelessly brazen, girl. What youngster would be so presumptuous as to believe that she could go from no music experience to ever becoming part of an established high school music program? It never occurred to me that I might not succeed in my unflinching belief.

Though I feel that Mr. Lee was a bit flummoxed, he did not openly challenge my plucky teenage behavior. He was too experienced for that. Instead, he got up and walked over to unlock a tall, metal cabinet. He removed a small black case and brought it over to our table. He popped the locks with his thumbs and opened the case to display a dinged-up, silver-colored metal clarinet. I expected to see a traditional black one. No matter. Mr. Lee was entrusting me with a real musical instrument. I didn't care what it looked like. I could hardly wait to hold it, which I did as he showed me how to put the reed on the mouthpiece and blow into it. He had me play each note on the scale to show me the fingerings that produced them. My insides quivered in excitement.

In retrospect, I believe Mr. Lee was challenging me with the runt of the litter (the dinged-up metal clarinet), so to speak, to make good on my bravado. If I could rise above the challenge of the runt, then I had a chance to succeed.

With the clarinet, he also gave me my first book of simple music to practice. I was so ready to play music, to practice, practice, practice.

I practiced every minute I could. My father disapproved of my need for music. To him, music was a waste. So, I practiced away from him. In the car in the driveway, with my music propped on the glove-box door. In the garage, where I leaned my music on the massive, grubby vise. I practiced inside only when my father was away from the house. But I practiced. And I struggled with producing strong, clean notes. The B flat was the worst. The runt was not going to do me in, however.

I was blessed that my father was a journeyman tool maker. This title meant that he was important in his job and often was expected to work overtime. Overtime kept him away from home for many extra hours nearly every day.

His increased absence was really welcome as the weather grew colder and the music more intricate and difficult. Cold fingers are too stiff to quickly play a line of sixteenth notes or many measures of sixteenth and eighth notes. Add to this challenge, my unskilled brain struggling to will my fingers to master the music. Playing inside absolutely facilitated my learning and my proficiency. This was helpful, because Mr. Lee continued to give me more-advanced, faster music to practice. I didn't really notice so much; I just played.

When I went for my lesson just before Christmas break, Mr. Lee walked over to that tall, metal filling cabinet and removed a shiny black case, the size of the case I had. He placed it on the table where we had our first conversation and popped the locks. There in the plush blue-black velvet lay a shiny black clarinet. I was so overwhelmed that I couldn't say a word. I'm sure Mr. Lee noticed the tears in my eyes, however.

"You have earned this." He said without fanfare. "Come to band practice on the Monday when we return from the holiday break. You will be sitting third chair." This is the equivalent of being the low player on the clarinet pecking order. "I'll take the instrument you have now when we finish today's lesson." Mr. Lee was a man who spoke important words only. We walked over to the practice area and today's lesson.

From June to December, I had become a member of the Northville High School Band. By the end of my time in the band, I had learned to play the alto and tenor saxophones and played tenor saxophone in the All District Band. I also had earned a music scholarship to Wayne State University in Detroit.

This brash country kid, with no music experience at all, marched into the Director's office with the strength of the Holy Spirit and the grace of God (prevenient grace) and came away with the challenge to become a band member. I did not understand about grace, but as I walked to the car, I believed the prize would be mine. Now, I understand. He had granted me the grace to own what I wanted with confidence.

Stories of Family Prevenient Grace

My stories, thus far, reflect how prevenient grace has shaped my life. Yet, I also have benefited vicariously from prevenient grace in my family's lives. What better way to understand just how strong is God's presence in one's life, one's whole life, than by showing God's all-inclusive prevenient grace to gain one's attention?

God has provided vignettes of significant events in the lives of two members of my family—my husband and one of my daughters. I am sure, however, that there may be others. He was doing His best to reach me. I hear tell that I am a tough nut to reach and even tougher to crack.

One other thing—as you read, you might think that God did not grant me any prevenient grace from high school until I was married and had children. That might be true. But because my marriage was within months of graduation, and our family began the next year, I probably was too busy with these significant transitions in my life to pay attention. I doubt that God had set me out on my own.

Them Bones, Them Bones

In the early 1970s, soon after we moved to Illinois, my husband, Ben, twisted his back at work. As with many men, if not most, he was inclined to "tough it out." Heaven forbid he should go to a doctor.

Nevertheless, the pain grew intense enough that it rolled over his tough-guy routine and flattened his resolve. The physician he finally consulted immediately referred him to an orthopedic surgeon.

A battery of tests determined that Ben needed surgery on his spine. Long story short, as they say, 15 years of hidden prevenient grace had brought my husband to the surgery that saved him from probable paralysis.

•. •. •. • •

PREVENIENT GRACE

Dr. Graham, the orthopedic surgeon, pushed open the double doors from the surgery wing, shaking his head as walked toward me. I stood and walked toward him. He pulled off his green surgical cap and ruffled his thinning hair.

"Your husband is one damn lucky man," he said, still shaking his head.

Surprised by his manner, I asked "Oh? Why is that?"

"Well, one vertebra was snapped in two. What makes him lucky is this: That vertebra was broken a long damn time ago, years ago. Probably playing football. He did play football, didn't he?"

"Yes, big time defensive player."

"Here's the thing," he continued. "The vertebrae protect the spinal column from injury. Basically, those two pieces of bone that should have been protecting his spinal column were floating around it, endangering the cord every minute of every day. Any 'just right' jostle or bump could have paralyzed him."

Dr. Graham kept looking at me, letting his message sink in. My husband had been a crisis waiting to happen for 15 years. I was speechless. To repair Ben's spine, Dr. Graham performed a spinal fusion with a sliver of bone from his Ben's hip and a laminectomy (the removal of the back of the vertebra). Ben would have no serious residual effect from the surgery, the doctor told me.

Ben was a big man. Six foot one, weighing about 250 pounds. He had played defense for his team at Bentley High in Livonia, MI from 1952 to 1956, when he graduated. We had no way of knowing when that injury had occurred. It didn't really matter. The possible life-changing experience had lingered only a block or a tackle away at any practice or on any given intense game day or routine practice during those years.

The slip-and-twist injury that prompted the surgery had been a moment of prevenient grace in his life. God presented the vignette to me many years later, after Ben's death from complications from a heart attack, as I began this book of prevenient-grace stories.

Ben and I were married in August 1956, and a lot of living occurred between then and his surgery in 1971. We had bowled and played badminton and volleyball with the family. We also created four children in those years, so he clearly was engaged in the baby-making and the child-rearing activities. For 15 years, Ben had lived a normal life with a broken vertebra that threatened his spinal cord and, ultimately, his mobility. More importantly, however, his slip-and-twist brought to light how long-term God's gift of prevenient grace can last.

He had preserved Ben's health until He decided that the time was right for the disclosure.

I understood at the time that Ben had been spared paralysis; I, on the other hand, had not yet understood that Ben's gift of health was one more spiritual breadcrumb.

Thanksgiving for Deliverance

Fear is not a word
That I would associate
With the Lord of Lords.

Reverence says more
About how you touch my soul
In my darkest hours.

I remain in awe
And humble obedience
In your renewed grace.

At first, I tremble.
Then my joyful spirit rises
And reverence reigns.

Please, Please, Not My Beautiful Little Girl

Sharon was living in her little-girl world behind big, blue-rimmed glasses. She was nearly five and had just started to wear glasses. Mostly, she didn't seem to mind them. From my perspective, they added to her individuality. I knew, though, that she would tell me later on how she felt about them.

She was an unassuming child who pretty much played in her own space, no matter what her younger brothers were doing. She didn't like to be bothered when she was playing.

On this particular morning, Sharon was playing with the pots and pans in the lower cupboards, while I worked in the kitchen. Her three-year-old brother, Tim, began to interfere with her play. She tried to chase him off, but he persisted. Finally, she picked up my Revere

Ware frying pan and beaned him with it. He was surprised, but his spirit was wounded much more than he was physically hurt. She had delivered a warning shot, not a full-on "take that!" blow. Nevertheless, a battle broke out.

As I calmed the warriors, I noticed some strange bumps on Sharon's arm. Smooth, under-the-skin bumps. A few smaller bumps also showed on her neck and face. "I have seen this before," I thought. The search of my brain images produced Mildred, an older woman in town, who was covered in bumps like these. Big one. Little ones. Bumps on virtually her whole body. That disconcerting image immediately popped into my mind as I surreptitiously inspected Sharon a little more carefully.

"Please, not my beautiful little girl," I thought, not wanting my Sharon to grow up with a physical distraction, such as Mildred's. My girl was a sensitive child to begin with. This affliction, which I learned was lipoma, fatty tumors under the skin, would really add to her feelings of being different because, well, she would be different. Oh, my, this certainly would complicate her life still more. I didn't call attention to the bumps when I separated the scrappers. It would be time enough to talk when she noticed them. My heart sank, and I just thought the words, "Please, not my beautiful little girl."

It was springtime, and Sharon lived mostly in her play world. She was not an inquisitive child. Life went on. I took the children out in the yard to play, and we went for walks. We visited with friends. We worked in the yard and tended my rose bushes. We found earthworms and grubs in the newly turned earth. We did all sorts of normal activities together, and I paid no notice to the fatty tumors. They were there, but not there, if you know what I mean. If I were fretful, then Sharon would become fretful, without understanding why. She took on the energy of someone else. Fretting accomplishes nothing. Fretting wastes energy.

Basically, I could do nothing about the disease. My doctor said that lipoma is a lifetime condition. I can't wish it away. There is no medication that diminishes Lipoma.

One day, when I scooped her up for a cuddle, I was stunned. The fatty tumors were gone. Absolutely gone. As I said, my doctor had told me that lipoma do not just go away. Nevertheless, her fatty tumors were gone. Not a single tumor of any size lingered anywhere.

It is possible, of course, that I didn't see what I thought I saw, but I am not given to hyperbole. Neither do I have a heightened imagination. Life for me then, as it is now, was that the here and the now are all that matters. I had helped support my family as a nonfiction-freelance writer. Later, I fully supported my family as a journalist, which definitely is a nonfiction endeavor. I see what I see, research the subject to make sure I know what I see, then report the who, what, where, when, why, and how to bring what I saw into focus.

In that place and time, in that glorious day, my Sharon had only her bright smile, big glasses, and very smooth skin. And God had granted me another clear example of prevenient grace.

The Little Old Lady in Sneakers

My four children and I were settling in at the boarding gate in O'Hare Airport in Chicago, awaiting departure to Moline, Illinois, the destination that would eventually take us to our new home.

Our arrival gate was only two gates from our departure gate, an unexpected but welcome blessing in air travel. This gift allowed us unhurried time for potty breaks, hand washing, freshening of faces, and a diaper change for my toddler.

It was midafternoon on a Thursday. Activity on the concourse was light and slow moving. I had planned our trip to avoid the bustle of the end-of-day business travelers. I also had wanted as little confusion as possible, traveling with small children. So far, all had gone well. We did experience a little dust-up with Tim in the first part of our trip, from Detroit to Chicago, but the fuss settled quickly.

Now, we had about 40 minutes before boarding. Laurie, my ten-year-old, went to a quieter area to read. Sharon, five, and Tim, three, were in front of me, choosing juice boxes from the bag on my lap. Dan, two, was standing next to me, fiddling with some small toys on the seat of the chair. I gratefully enjoyed this moment of slow time.

A moment was all it was, however.

Suddenly, Dan turned from his toys and bolted out into the concourse, running as fast as his chubby little legs would move. I shoved the stuff off my lap, onto the floor and told the kids to "Stay Here!" I dashed off in Dan's direction of travel. I could see him, easily. The flow of humanity on the concourse had parted like the Red Sea and let my Dan run and run.

It was 1967, and travel clothing was dressy. Not Sunday-best dress, but definitely not hanging-out clothes, either. I wore a slim-fitting pencil skirt, with its generous two-inch vent at the hem, and pointy toed shoes with two-inch heels. My appropriate attire seriously hampered pursuit of my not-so-toddling toddler. I also was a shy person in those days and would not have kicked off shoes or shouted at my child to stop. So, I did my best at hurrying. I wished, too, that Dan's little feet would get ahead of themselves and he would lose his balance. Not a chance. He just kept running. I know that running had to feel good to him. We had been inside and behaving ourselves far too long for all of the children. If I could have, I know that I would have run, just to feel free.

Enter the fabled "little old lady in tennis shoes." I kid you not. This older woman, short and sort of bent over, with thinning white hair and wearing a print dress and sneakers, appeared from among the travelers. She reached out and snatched my runaway by the strap on his white shorts with the red and blue boats on them.

Grabbing the thin strap on a moving child was a feat of skill all its own. She brought Dan up short. The abrupt stop made his eyes get big.

"I thought you needed a little help," she said, as she handed him off to me, smiling sweetly. I thanked her, several times. I would have hugged her if I hadn't been so concerned that my blond-haired, innocent-looking boy child would escape again. The crowd was enjoying every moment of Dan's adventure and my consternation.

As I turned us around to head back to our boarding area, I looked back to wave or smile or give some kind of parting gesture that would show my gratefulness one more time. The little old lady was gone. No old woman, anywhere. No gaily colored print dress anywhere among the people on the wide-open concourse. Only men in suits and women in business dress.

Later, I thought about how my helpful little old woman had just appeared when I needed someone to help me. I laughed to myself. I had not been one to believe in angels or God showing up in a print dress, but then, I was not so sure. Poof! There she was. Poof! There she wasn't.

An Abrupt Turn of Events

The vignette for this recollection of prevenient grace came as a picture of me shivering wildly in an old-fashioned, metal, crib-like hospital bed. A strange machine hissed and thumped somewhere to the left of me in the dimly lit room. "I was with you" whispered in my ear.

"How're you doing this morning, Mrs. Foor?" It was a little after 8 a.m., and the day nurse was making her rounds.

"Well, Mrs. Potts," I said, as I squinted at her name badge to see who was talking to me, "All things considered, I am doing reasonably okay."

"And what does 'reasonably okay' mean?"

"It means that you are the fifth shift of nurses I have spoken to, and I still am pregnant and in labor."

"How about your labor?"

"How about that labor thing?" I said, in sarcasm as I breathed through a stiff contraction. "I have been at this for what, nearly two days, and I still am not in delivery. The contractions are stronger, but not strong enough to get the job done. This is my fifth child, and I know what productive labor feels like."

"As soon as I finish my med rounds, I'll give your doctor a call."

Not long after that conversation, labor began with zeal. I let the nurse's station know. Before long, an unfamiliar doctor and nurse came in. No introduction. No names. My nurse said, in her stage-direction voice, that he was an obstetrics specialist, here to check on my progress. Perish the thought that he should notice that I am a real person and might like to know his name. I can tell you, with painful certainty, that being examined vaginally in the middle of a contraction is, I imagined, the equivalent of having a root canal without lidocaine. Breath-taking.

Dr. No Name straightened up, ripped off his gloves, and directed my nurse to "call OR and tell them to ready for a C-section. Now!" He directed the other nurse to get 20 ccs of some drug. "And get some help in here. Now!" For some reason, the end of my bed had been elevated by blocks under its wheels the day before. He kicked the blocks out of the way, and my bed banged onto the floor. As this happened, a nurse jammed a syringe full of something into my thigh. A couple of extra men showed up, and they began to maneuver my bed through the doorway and into the hall. I couldn't tell if they were running, but it surely felt like it. I tried to look at the ceiling, but my eyes were . . .

•. •. •. • •

"Can you hear me, Mrs. Foor?" A hand gently squeezed my shoulder. "Open your eyes, Mrs. Foor. If you can hear me, just say 'Yes.'"

"Yes," my thick tongue said through my cottonmouth. I could hear the disembodied voices and activity all around me, but what the heck had happened from my doorway to this bed?

Well, long story short, as they say, I was, at that moment, beginning my recovery from an emergency cesarean section. The examination had revealed that the umbilical cord was wrapped across my baby's head. Every contraction stopped the flow of blood to his little body. A natural delivery endangered my baby's life and normal survival. As stunning as this revelation was, the worst was yet to come.

I saw my infant son three times before I developed a fever of 102 to 104. The fever kept my son in the nursery. They didn't know what was wrong with me, and they couldn't risk his contracting some illness from me. Delirium and violent chills soon accompanied the fever. Infant Jonathan went home with my neighbor, because I had disappeared into a near-death condition. Sometime, in the 30 hours before the urgent C-section, my water had broken, and the birth canal lay open to all manner of germy junk. As a result, I had developed septicemia, blood poisoning, which accounted for the fever and chills. Clearly, the oral drugs had been insufficient.

After some painful probing, a nurse finally found a vein in my left arm for an IV to carry intense doses of an antibiotic. In my stupor, the name of the drug sounded like "geranium," but I knew that probably was incorrect. Geraniums were what my Grandmother Kent raised in big pots on the round table in her front window. My brain wasn't working, and the irrelevant name floated around in my mind.

The nurse bound my forearm to a board, so I would not/could not dislodge the needle from my vein. This was 1972, and IVs came with long metal needles that slid into a vein. (No plastic butterfly needle advantage in those days.) To maintain the IV's usefulness, the site was immobilized. On a real board (maybe 1/2-inch thick x 4 inches wide) from my elbow to my fingers, which gripped the end of the board.

While my body lurched between chills and fever, my right leg began to hurt. Then it pained, even to move it slightly. I called my nurse and asked her to take a look. She did. She spoke not a word and walked away. Within minutes a doctor came in, pulled back the covers, and told my nurse to get in touch with my doctor "now!" There was that "now" imperative again. When the nurse returned with an oral drug to ease the pain, I asked her to prop pillows next to the outside of my leg.

The pain was so great with any movement, even to relax and let my leg loll to the side, made me to hold my breath. The pain exceeded the 10 on the normal 1-10 scale. Another specialist, Dr. Stiegel, the preeminent thoracic surgeon in our three-county area, was called in. (I know this about him because the columnist with whom I worked at *The Daily Dispatch*, was country-club buddies with him, and, as far as she was concerned, this doctor walked on water.) I had interrupted his July 4 weekend. Oh, my. The prospect of his equally important bill, to come sometime in the future, chilled my chills still more.

Before Dr. Stiegel arrived, I asked my nurse to help me sit up. I wanted to see why my leg hurt so damn much.

I was almost sorry I had done this. My leg had swelled to half again its normal size. Furthermore, it was an ugly purple log that lay lump-like next to my normal leg.

•. •. •. • •

Dr. Steigel came through the door, greeted me, and introduced himself as he pulled back the covers to expose my grotesque leg. He was contrary to my preconceived notion. I had expected to see a tall imposing figure, but Dr. Steigel was a stocky compact model with a crew cut. He gently palpated the length of the purpleness. As gentle as he tried to be, his touch sent sharp pains through my leg.

"Well, Mrs. Foor," he said as he took a deep breath, "you have a massive blood clot," with no kindly preamble. He pulled open the drawer in my bedside stand and removed the phone book. (Yes, in those days hospitals had phone books in their bedside stands.) He plopped the large book on my bed.

"Pick your funeral home, Mrs. Foor, because if you don't improve significantly within the next 24 hours, one of two things will happen: you will be leaving here with a toe tag, or I will be seeing you in surgery, at which time I will tie off your vena cava . . ."

PREVENIENT GRACE

I don't recall what he said after that. My attention seized after the words "toe tag." Between the chills, the fever, and the leg pain that was as much attention as I could muster.

"If you experience the feeling of anxiety, call your nurse. It could mean that the clot is moving." He added as he squeezed my shoulder and left my room.

Anxiety? What does anxiety feel like? I cannot recall ever feeling anxious about anything. And if the clot breaks free and heads toward my lungs or my brain, what can anyone do about it? Shove a finger into a vein to stop what one cannot see? Besides that, if the clot decides to relocate, I probably would be dead before the nurse could answer the bell.

I had what was called "milk leg" in the "olden days," before modern medicine and the three-day hospital stay. In those days, a woman would deliver her baby and spend a week in bed. Blood clots would form as a result of the inactivity. A woman could die just as easily as she could live. Death was pretty common among older women. I was 34 years old, and I had not been out of bed for more than a week. Hence, the blood clot.

When I first became so ill, my parish priest administered the Last Rites. I think that was supposed to make everything okay for me. Or would it? I was so sick at that point, I could not recall the formula for confession, and I mumbled something to get through it. When was my last confession? Had I ever made one? I couldn't remember. Would the priest's words and oils make a difference if I had not done my part correctly? The violent chills returned. My metal crib-like bed rattled fiercely. When the chills subsided, I fell asleep.

•. •. •. • •

I awoke in a fog. A strange feeling enveloped me, and I experienced a different kind of chill. Was this the feeling of anxiety that Dr. Steigel warned me of? Call the nurse, I thought. Why? She can't help me. If I am going to die, then I am going to die.

As I lay there sorting my thoughts, it seemed that someone was in my room. I had not heard anyone. I squinted through my nearsightedness. No one was there. Only the I-Vac machine from the intensive-care unit that relentlessly pumped heparin into my vein stood next to my bed. It hissed on the up stroke and "whumped" at the end of the downstroke. It was rhythmic, like listening to a machine breathing. No human was present, but the room still felt full of an enormous, imposing presence.

PREVENIENT GRACE

As whacko as it might sound, it felt like the presence moved. Suddenly, it occurred to me that the Holy Spirit was with me. That seemed a bit far-fetched, however. I was just an ordinary woman up to her ears in trouble after a not-so-routine birth. That thought gave me another chill, and the fever returned.

"Okay, God." I rasped aloud. "If it's really you here, I know that you can take my life in the next breath. But if I have a say in this, I can't leave just now. I have four children out there somewhere and a newborn in the care of my neighbor. You certainly know their father, and you know my children need me."

The presence drifted away. Like the bursting of a bubble. No sound. Just the release of tension. The containment was over. I believe that God gave me a choice: fight for your life or die. It's up to you.

My chills and fever left just as abruptly as the presence. I lay there wondering what had just happened. I felt alive again. I rang for my nurse.

Mrs. Potts was back on duty. She looked at me, kind of warily. She checked my vital signs, which were totally normal. "How do you feel?" She asked.

"I feel very tired, but other than that, I feel great." Mrs. Potts continued to look askance. I didn't tell her that I thought the Holy Spirit had visited me. I believed that had been the case, but the edge of disbelief lingered. If the experience was too much for my mind to embrace, it might be too much for her to digest, too. She might be alarmed and think that I had gone around the bend, into a new malady. I said only, "Thank God that's over."

No toe tag, no surgery. Just a long recovery.

For the next three weeks, I continued to need others to accomplish every basic function in my life.

Both arms had been immobilized with tape on boards to prevent movement of the intravenous needle that pumped the life-saving, clot-dissolving heparin, the left for massive doses of infection-killing drugs. Since then, nurses had to feed me, bathe me, and wipe my backside, anything and everything we take for granted.

Once the confinement was over, and I was given some freedom, I walked and walked and walked. I walked the hall in my ward and walked the hall in the next ward, until someone busted me.

•. •. •. • •

My survival in this story is paramount, but the good in this story of prevenient grace is not over.

I was admitted to Moline Public Hospital on June 19, 1972, my baby was born on June 21, and I was discharged on July 31. In those 43 days, I received an abundance of intensive care and special equipment in a surgical-care room because I could not be moved. Dr. Stiegel came for a visit, "just to see how you are doing," every day from July 3 until I was ambulatory, about four weeks later.

I could see bankruptcy in our future. My husband was still recovering from back surgery and my job, my first job since I was teenager, would not provide insurance coverage for a few more days.

On the days that the hospital bill and the specialist's bill arrived, I braced for the overwhelming numbers. I read the bills in disbelief. The hospital bill was slightly over $4,000 for the 43 days of delivery, baby care, and my intensive care. Math never was my strong suit, but I think that is just under $100 a day for specialized care for 43 days

Dr. Stiegel's bill, the bill I dreaded from the preeminent thoracic surgeon, was a total of $25 dollars for his month of stopping by to "see how you are doing."

And, still, I did not understand about God's grace until more than 50 years later.

The Mentor Most Mysterious

Not to put too fine a point on this prevenient-grace story, but it embraces many pieces of evidence of God's spiritual breadcrumbs, those silent times when God uses another person to direct His grace into the life of another to draw that person to Him. A woman, new to my life, passed along His gift of grace at several important junctures in a critical point in my life and that of my family.

Not long ago, I was writing a story for the regular readers of Stories Foortold about my being unsuited to becoming a pilot. My mind flashed on Dorothy Buresh, a writer at *The Daily Dispatch* in Moline IL home of the flight school. Once the door opened to the memory, the scenes of her presence in my early days of journalism overwhelmed.

PREVENIENT GRACE

Becoming a journalist had not been a choice; it was a necessity. My husband was out of work and recovering from spinal surgery, we were on food stamps and welfare, and we had five children. I needed a job. Most troubling in my search was the fact that I had no previous employment experience. During my "Mom days," I had dabbled in freelance writing, which allowed me to stay at home bring in a little money. My hobby became my family's salvation.

Elaine, the correspondent for *The Daily Dispatch* in our small community of Orion, IL, had read one of my stories in a regional magazine. Over the years, we had become friends. Our paths crossed at the post office one morning. She wondered if I had any story ideas.

"Yeah. I have one. The other day, my daughter mentioned that the PE (physical education) department was instituting a dance program for seniors."

"Dance classes for senior students?"

"That's what she said. And the students <u>must</u> show up for class every Monday through the semester."

"Why don't you pitch that story to Bill?" (Bill McElwain was editor of the features department.)

I was surprised. "You're their writer. Why don't you pitch it? I don't mind."

"Because you are a good writer," she replied, "and you need a regular job, don't you?"

89

"Well, I certainly do. Can't lie about that."

"Besides that, I have a feeling that Bill will bring you on as a full-time features writer." She smiled and turned toward her car.

Because I was in a desperate situation, I summoned my elusive courage and made an appointment with Mr. McElwain. "Your correspondent, Elaine, said I should come to you with this story," I told him, and I then explained the story to him in his office, as we talked about many topics.

Long story short, he pulled a Writer's Acceptance form from a drawer, told me that I would be paid for my story, and then said, "Go do it!"

The pay was minimal, but, bigger than the pay, my byline would be in the newspaper that my neighbors read. After I had made the arrangements with the authorities at Orion High School, I called Mr. McElwain, so that he could schedule a photographer. A professional photographer? Oh, wow!

Well, Mr. McElwain loved the story and scheduled it for the Sunday magazine section. Enter Dorothy Buresh, the same Dorothy Buresh who writes the beloved column *Battered Beat*, stories about anything and everything in Moline and its people. She also helped Mr. McElwain with the magazine.

PREVENIENT GRACE

When she called me at home to go over some details, she told me how much she enjoyed my dance-class story, but (must there always be a "but") . . . "Where are the cutlines?"

I was startled. "Cutlines? What are cutlines?" I had never heard that term.

On the other end of the conversation, Mrs. B sighed. Heavy. Noisy. Impatient. "Those lines under a photo that explain what the photo is about, do you read them?" She sounded rather testy.

"Yes." I replied, fearing that anything beyond that might aggravate her still more.

"Those are called cutlines." More sighing. "I need them for the photos that will accompany your story. Just write them. I will handle the technicalities. I need them by tomorrow afternoon." She hung up.

I had copies of the three photos and wrote the cutline for each that night. I delivered them early the next morning, hoping to impress Mrs. Buresh. I rapped on her office door. "Good morning, Mrs. Buresh." I tried to sound confident, upbeat.

"First of all," she said, "Don't call me 'Mrs. Buresh.' Sounds old, and I am not old. Call me Dorothy. Everyone else does." Testy must be her mood of choice. I was bemused.

Had me fooled at that age thing, she did. Dorothy, in her late 50s to early 60s, stood about 5 feet 6 inches tall, with a motherly build. In contrast to the other women in the news department, she wore an ordinary but nice green-print dress that suited her and, as Grandmother would say, "hose and serviceable shoes." Her salt-and-pepper gray hair, as I would learn in our association, was perpetually "tousled." Her voice conveyed some age. Nonetheless, this collection of details only affirmed that Dorothy Buresh was well in charge of this moment and all that came after. She had that strong country feel about her. Having lived small-town country most of my life, I recognized a trustworthiness in her. Or believed that I had.

Mr. McElwain, Bill, did hire me full-time in the features department. And Dorothy shepherded this journalistic greenhorn through her many inadequacies in a half dozen feature stories. The rest of the time, I wrote filler pieces, short items about newsworthy factoids.

Within a few months, I was summarily transferred to the Women's Department. I was unsure why this changed had occurred. I also was unaware of the rivalry between Bill and my new editor. Bill had me, she wanted me, she got me. Until then, office politics had escaped my attention.

PREVENIENT GRACE

I was dismayed that I had been conscripted to the Nine Circles of Hell that was the Women's Department and in the control of the Queen Bee. I had no idea on which circle I existed, maybe fraud or treachery, but it didn't matter. Hell is hell. This woman could have been the model for Cruella De Vil. Thin, pinched, unsmiling face, threatening tone of voice. I had learned about the "Queen Bee syndrome" in management classes, now I was learning its truth, up close and real personal.

I was low person on her totem pole. She didn't particularly want me, a commoner, in her department, but she now had what Bill had had—me. The Queen Bee and her husband, a lump in the newspaper's all-male management team, were part of the country-club set and lived on the correct side of town. I, on the other hand, lived in a hayseed farming town. She believed, and treated me as such, that I was unschooled, maybe even ignorant, a mere housewife, and, now, a modern-day slave to further her image of being a good editor.

From my perspective, Cruella wielded her judgement as though she were a Society Editor. When she plopped wedding and engagement forms next to my typewriter, the forms specified what size headline to put on each. Commoners received 24-point headlines, "names" received the larger 30-point headlines and head shots. No head shots for commoners.

I inquired why we did that. "One woman's wedding or engagement is as important to her as that of another woman."

"Because some women are more important than others," she told me, a menacing sneer and glint in her eye. Never brought up that topic again. After that exchange, I decided that I had obediently written about Chantilly lace, finger-tip length sleeves, tiaras and other such nonsense for way too long. Still, I was too new to change my circumstances.

Dorothy and I crossed paths in the hallway to the Ladies room one day. She stopped me and surveyed our area, hugger-mugger style. "Do you want to stay in the Women's Department?" She inquired in a conspiratorial tone of voice, watching my eyes, assessing my attitude. Her question and demeanor said she also was assessing my integrity.

"No." My answer was firm. "I am not into discrimination. Writing it or living it."

Dorothy smiled. "That's good because the Queen Bee will chew you up, spit you out, and stomp on your bones."

My assessment exactly. Conversation over. Dorothy pushed open the Ladies room door.

That had been a curious exchange. She was correct, but, in truth, I still was too new to rock my employment boat. My family needed me to bring home the grocery money, so I remained quiet and subservient.

One morning, Russ, the managing editor, called me into his office. That was a scary invitation. The managing editor supervises the entire news operation and its employees. "You need to gain some new experiences, " he said, among some complementary things, and transferred me out of hell and into the newsroom to report on the life and the times in a couple of neighboring communities. I was a reporter, a minor one to be sure, but I no longer served as Cruella's minion.

I was ecstatic! I had my own designated space in the drama of daily news. Manual typewriter, scissors, glue pot, and all. In those days, reporters produced copy on long pieces of newsprint. For example, if I needed to change anything in my story, I literally had to cut the offending copy from the rest and paste the good stuff in its place. The best part of being in the newsroom, however, was that I could see who was who and who did what. I learned a lot about Dorothy.

Again, much later in my days at *The Daily Dispatch*, our paths crossed in the hallway at the Ladies room. "You been doing alright?" I was beginning to wonder whether these were planned meetings.

"Sure. It's interesting but a bit slow. To tell you the truth, I wish I could edit some of this copy. These guys can't spell, and they use incorrect words." Dorothy laughed. Conversation over. Poof. She disappeared into the Ladies room. Days later, I was unceremoniously assigned to our bureau office in Cambridge as an assistant editor.

Now, as grateful as I was for the advancements and the experience, they unnerved me. This was my first job outside of my home, and I was unsure about protocols and such. I tried to stay out of trouble and hold my tongue—a troublesome chore, even 50 years ago. Every time they gave me a new assignment, I wondered whether they were laying a trap, trying to get me to screw up so they could fire me. I couldn't afford to lose this job. My family needed to feel safe, with food and a home.

Before I left the main office for Cambridge, the newsroom had converted to the first version of computer-generated copy. Each one of us now produced optical-scanner-ready copy on IBM Selectric typewriters. That process was equal to being a minion in Cruella's hell.

Cutting and pasting was just a bother compared to this puzzle of symbols. The writer had to insert funny little symbols in a line of typing to tell the scanner that the next line of type would replace the type that went before. The beginning of the deletion also had its funny little symbol. It was pain in my soul to deal with and impossible to explain here.

One afternoon, as Dorothy struggled to complete her column under this new system, the tedious-but-necessary process had driven her to the last scintilla of patience. She bellowed a stream of words that would have withered the most seasoned of stevedores and grabbed ahold of her IBM. She continued her rip-roaring verbal assault on computers and the cumbersome process and then, with raw determination, she began to lift the IBM monster.

Every man in the newsroom ran, I mean RAN, to intercede. In her frustration and anger, Dorothy raged in an adrenaline high and would have destroyed this very expensive typewriter if Jim, the city editor, had not grabbed the machine and stopped her. Together, they set the typewriter down. I still can see and hear her, even now.

It's important that I not leave you with that scene in mind. As I have written this story, the images of those days have come together. They were only bits and bobs as I lived them then. I was so intent upon doing my best job because I was out of my league in these circumstances. I was Mother Hubbard with a cupboard so bare and a soul in despair. I was so focused on avoiding unseen pitfalls that I had failed to notice so much, particularly Dorothy's influence on my behalf.

Dorothy and I never became friends, but we were friendly acquaintances. Given what I understand about her now, she was watching over me and guiding my progress out of this toxic situation. Cruella routinely gave me the "eye" and a bit of smart mouth as she passed. The Queen Bee had lost her control of my circumstances. I cannot prove any of what I believe; I just feel its truth in my heart and soul.

Although Dorothy seemed rather ordinary in the newsroom, formidable but ordinary, there was not an important personage in the community whom she did not greet warmly on a first-name basis. The return greetings were just as genuine and just as warm.

I believe also, though cannot prove, that I benefitted from her watchfulness, her inimitable persuasion, and her incredible contacts at a very precarious time in my life. As I wrote in *An Abrupt Turn of Events,* I had spent 43 days under critical care and constant attention in the public hospital where Dorothy's dear friend, Marguerite (I believe that was her name), was administrator. The bill for those 43 days without insurance? Just over $4,000.

PREVENIENT GRACE

Dorothy and her husband also regularly dined with the pre-eminent thoracic surgeon in the state and his wife. The same surgeon who had been called in on my case at Marguerite's hospital. When Dr. Steigel came to my room for the consultation, on July 4, he stirred my adrenalin with the words "toe tag," words that scared me into working to get better. Dr. Steigel stopped in every day for some 17 days "just to see how you're doing." His bill? An unbelievable $25.

Dorothy daily lived among the A Listers. She lunched with them, dined with them, enjoyed them on a first-name basis. In addition to the hospital administrator and the prominent surgeon were the owners of John Deere, the mayor of Moline, and virtually every councilman with whom she chose to share her table.

To my mind, the most joyful thing about Dorothy Buresh, the beloved columnist, is that she unabashedly owned and relished every molecule of her being. She coupled her unassuming demeanor with the grace of her humanity. No matter the size of her home, her financial status, or the people with whom she shared time, her dignified spiritual presence spoke eloquently for her.

Unnoticed in her generosity of spirit at the time, Dorothy had guided this greenhorn's path through the briar patch of journalism with aplomb and grace. Her guidance gave me the foundation upon which my family and I have survived.

I respected her then. Her memory is even more dear.

Words of Absolute Praise

No eye can avoid
The wholeness of your presence,
Your abundant love.

Your living water
Spills restorative power
To all precious life.

Your gifts humble me
And stir me to serve you more.
I await your word.

God Has a Sense of Humor

I have included these next stories because I believe God has a sense of humor and sometimes a playful side. I believe this because we are created in His image. Therefore, we have a sense of humor as He has a sense of humor. He sometimes likes to test our adaptability, our ability to trust, and I believe he uses humor to teach as we use it.

The situation in each of these stories could have resulted in ugliness of one kind or another. However, in retrospect and with a greater understanding of God, I believe that He was testing me in a fun kind of way. Heaven knows, He has tested my resilience in more serious situations. A bit of fun certainly couldn't hurt, now could it.

The first story, I Need A Jeep, took place in the late 1960s. The other, I Forgot to Check the Thyme, occurred about 10 years ago.

I Need a Jeep

God knew that I was up to the challenge of owning this well-aged vehicle. He could have prevented my husband from buying it, but He didn't. Instead, He teased me along in good humor, letting my children in on the fun and waiting for me to catch on and take care of business. I believe this because I never felt fearful about these mishaps. I was sort of in on the joke, but I wasn't. I did enjoy my Jeep's little foibles.

This is a story about a car. Not just any car, but a Jeep Wagoneer from the 1960s. Why is this vehicle so important to my life? Although the Jeep has a storied history in wartime, this Wagoneer began to wage war on me.

My husband, Ben, ever the romantic, thought that my comments about wanting a Jeep should be taken seriously. Mostly, I muttered how a Jeep would be a more appropriate vehicle to transport our children to various social obligations over the oil-covered country roads.

Towns with barren, dusty country roads kept the dust down by spreading waste oil on the roadway. The tires on one's vehicle spewed oil up and onto the sides of the vehicle. Driving with the right-side wheels on the grassy shoulder cut the mess in half, but it still was one daunting muck-up that would eat the paint off one's vehicle if the oil were left on it for any length of time.

Anyway, Betty, the florist in our little farming town of Orion, IL, was giving up her business, and she was selling her delivery wagon. It was 1970, and in the intervening years, Betty had delivered years' worth of wedding flowers and funeral wreaths and untold bouquets of prom and anniversary arrangements in that Wagoneer. The community counted on Betty to deliver. Deliver she did. As a result, her dependable Wagoneer was as tired as she.

Ben was so proud of his purchase, but I just knew from our history that this "gift" would, at some point, become a misadventure in a red bow. The Wagoneer was built to be a utilitarian work-oriented vehicle. It looked like a boxy station wagon, with plenty of room for children and their sporting equipment or whatever.

And the oil would lay its foul blackness on the aging work vehicle, not on the family sedan.

My Wagoneer was a very plain white. Nondescript as vehicles go. The kids were excited about having a different kind of vehicle, a fun vehicle, to ride in. They were, that is, until I installed the gaudy pink seat covers with dinner-plate sized white flowers for a little pizazz. What did they expect? These seat covers were, after all, the best and the most distinctive the auto parts store had to offer. How could I resist? At that point, the children started asking me to drop them off well before the school yard, even in our miserable, inclement weather. That was their choice. A little extra time in the tough weather could build character, give them something to think about.

We weathered this battle, so to speak, between my choice of bright seat covers and their decisions for early drop off, but then, I was faced with new challenges. My Wagoneer turned against me.

For openers, the kids and I were on our way out of town on U.S.150. We were in the midst of an ugly, persistent rainstorm. The wipers were whipping back and forth at high speed. Back and forth, back and forth, sweeping sheets of water from the windshield. Suddenly, the wiper blade on the passenger side whipped off into the ditch. I still had a working blade on my side of the vehicle, but full vision was gone. I slowed down and looked for a safe zone to pull off the road and wait for a respite in the rain. Nice idea, but the wrong place to find such a place. I'm driving in rural Illinois, which is nothing but miles and miles of fence lines and the occasional sideroad, which I could not see in time to turn safely. So, I kept driving until a gas station provided some space to stop. I got some gas while I was there.

The rain stopped fairly soon, and I decided to return to Orion, rather than continue to the nonessential destination in Galesburg. My friend would just have to wait until I got home to know that I was safe but would not be at her house today. The kids were in the car, and for all I knew, the rain might return, and the wiper blade on my side might also end up in a ditch. For that matter, I was too frazzled for a replay of the stress.

For all the drama of that day, the Wagoneer was not quite done with me. In the days to come, the engine started misfiring. The engine would "take a breath," when I hit a bump. Then, the engine would stop a bit, hesitate, and then start breathing again. Bump. Take a breath. Breathe again. The whole thing was a bother, but not enough to stop me.

Then, I had been assigned to interview the owners of the Osco Fireworks Company (now Nostalgia Fireworks) for the Fourth of July tabloid. The fireworks factory was new and the only fireworks maker in Illinois. My jeep and I are cruising along on this well-maintained concrete country road. No traffic; just feeder cattle and seed corn to the right and left of me. Speed limit is 45 mph.

I took the railroad crossing a little too fast for its condition. The crossing had not been well maintained, so when I hit the jumble of construction material and ruts that passed for the track bed, the engine flat out stopped. I was startled. Fortunately, the momentum carried me across the tracks.

This was not a little stopping of the engine. It was a major stopping of breath, and the stunning engine silence made me catch my breath. Adrenaline rushed through my extremities, big time. I was unsure that the engine would start breathing again, but it did. Augie and Earl, the town's mechanics who were wizards with broken cars and trucks, were in my future for the afternoon.

Vehicles in those days had distributors and rotors. No computers. Just wires and parts that held the wires and spark plugs in place and ensured the even distribution of the electrical current. Well, when Augie removed the distributor cap, he started laughing. I peered over his shoulder. He pointed to the main distributor wire. It was broken from the distributor post and was just laying loose on the distributor body. The engine had continued to operate because the electrical current from the plugs arced from the broken wire to the distributor. That the arcing current kept the engine running was evidenced by the deep, black scorch mark on the hub. Every time I hit a bump, the fragile arcing connection also was broken, and the engine stopped.

After that revelation, my Mr. Romantic decided that he needed to get rid of the Wagoneer before he lost a wife. I don't know how or where that fun little experiment in gift-giving went, but my life in the country lost a little of its adventure.

I Forgot to Check the Thyme

Don't even start this story if you have a thing about snakes because a baby milk snake is the star of this moment of prevenient grace.

I was talking with a friend and walking around with the portable phone. I had just returned home from a vacation with friends in North Carolina and was checking in. Out of the corner of my eye, I caught a glimpse of slight movement in the hallway to my bedroom. I continued talking and walked carefully closer to the movement.

Oh, good grief! It's snake! A baby snake! "Uh, Doris? Igottahangupgoodbye." I didn't give her time to reply. I laid the phone on the desk next to me.

The colorful, six-inch critter was stealthily, steadily moving along the 12-foot stretch of white baseboard and blue carpet toward my room. It was almost like he was watching, maybe expecting another snake to jump out at him and holler "Boo!"

What could I find that was long enough and strong enough to stop him? My mind raced through the possibilities. Ah! My hiking stick! I ran to get it from the corner in the kitchen, praying that the snake was continuing in its slow manner. All movement down that hallway was negative, from my point of view, but slow progress was good.

I returned with the hiking stick and moved slowly behind my intruder, looking for the right place to pound the stick on him. A place that would allow me to make the stop, rather than exciting him into rapid movement directly into my bedroom, if I missed.

Oh, good grief! Good grief! I kept thinking. I'm not afraid of snakes, but I really don't like the fact that they curl around your hand, your arm, any part of you. Reminds me of the worms I tried to impale with the hook when I went fishing with my uncle. Flip, flop, flip, flop. Flip around my finger. And I would throw the whole thing in the air or into the water. Eeew!

At first, I had thought the markings resembled those of the deadly coral snake. From a distance, its markings seemed to be those of the coral snake. I'm sure I thought of the coral snake because Doris and I had been talking about snakes of the mountains and the difference between the coral snake and its look alike the king snake. We had scoffed, laughed at the cute but confusing rhymes that have been devised to help people tell the difference between the two. It seemed just as easy, from our point of view, to simply know that the coral snake has a threatening black head; the king snake, on the other hand, is just a sassy red head.

Our rocking-chair conversation probably was guiding my thoughts as I watched this particular snake continue to slowly slink toward my bedroom. Yet, as I stalked the critter, I realized that the markings were different. I didn't stop to ask myself whether young snakes are differently marked from adults as young birds so frequently are. This was no time for one of my thoughtful evaluations, however.

I admit that I also was intrigued by the snake's attitude. He must have been scared. He didn't know where he was, and, maybe, if he just moved slowly, no one would notice him. His movement was almost imperceptible, so straight and deliberate as he hugged the baseboard that he could have been pulled along on a string.

Oh, good grief! Dang it! My mind vacillated between moments of science-like observations and questions and the need to get the creature out of my house. Now!

Then, the time was right! I smacked the end of the hiking stick down onto him. I missed his head, which was my target, but I got 'em. He was stopped but not done.

I hate to kill things. Or even hurt them. Life is life, and I wouldn't want someone to pin me to the floor while I writhed around scared and hurt like he probably was. Killing him wasn't as possible as one might think. My hiking stick has a rubber tip on it for stability in smooth places, and he was on a well-padded carpet. He was between a piece of rubber and a soft place.

I, on the other hand, stood between the rock and the hard place. I was alone. I had stopped a snake that still was alive. I was not about to pick up the critter because it would surely do the flipflopflipflop, curl thing, and then I would just throw it all in the air and have to start over. Only then, the snake, scared into action, would be moving at snake speed. Not a wise move on my part, I decided.

To add to my dilemma, I had left the phone on the desk. Five feet away.

Oh, good grief! (My exclamations are limited. I am not a curse-word person.)

I thought a moment. Then, I wedged the stick firmly into the corner of the door frame and on top of the snake. I kept watch as I dashed for the phone. I dialed Ron, my son-in-law, who lives a short distance away. Sort of around the corner, so to speak. Sharon, my daughter, answered. Ron was in bed and asleep. I told her what was going on. She said she would wake him. I knew she would try to do that because she *really* doesn't like snakes.

I stood there, my hand tightly holding the stick, waiting patiently, wishing this disturbance was over, worrying about the condition of the unsuspecting intruder. Before too long, I heard the kitchen door open. The kids all have keys to the house, which meant I didn't have to leave my post to let Ron in.

Sharon, not Ron, came around the corner. She was there because Ron was sound asleep and because she knew I needed only a second pair of hands, not someone to slay my dragon. Nevertheless, she wasn't the least bit happy about playing any part in this drama.

She awaited directions. I told her to come and hold the stick. She did so, as far away from our visitor as her long arm would reach. The snake continued to wiggle around. I hurried to get my work gloves off the potting bench on the porch. I can do anything when I am wearing my work gloves. Lift heavy weights with edges that normally would press into my tender flesh. Crush the seals on cardboard boxes. And I can slay dragons, especially tiny ones such as this, with my hands, if I must. I returned, hands in work gloves, ready to dispose of this hapless baby. Sharon held the stick steady while I got a hold on the snake's head. Once I had done that, I grabbed his body, and Sharon moved the stick. She didn't exactly run when I picked him up, but it was a good imitation, hopping and jumping out of the way.

In a speedy trip through the kitchen and out the door, and then outside while Sharon held open the porch door, I flung my unwanted visitor into the night. If he wasn't dead, he probably wished he was. He had been through 30 minutes of hell, and now he was hurtling through the darkness and would land he knew not where. Sharon said it looked like I was trying to throw him to Tampa. but I think he landed somewhere in my yard. I have no idea why I threw him. It would have been more humane to set him down in the soil under the juniper bushes to let him regroup, but, no, I threw him. He probably died of fright or some other terrible affliction. I felt bad; Sharon, not so much.

How did that snake get into the house? I do not leave outside doors open. Particularly, how did a baby snake end up in my house? After the hubbub settled, I consulted my snake identification book. It was a milk snake, which is a species of the king snake. (Yes, I really do have an identification book for snakes. And for birds, spiders, butterflies, and fish.)

Did I have anything new in my environment that would accommodate this snake? I thought for a moment. Yes! I did, as a matter of fact. Several big, healthy, potted parsley, rosemary, thyme, and basil plants came home with me. The baby snake could have been in there, riding down from the mountains with me. A couple of snails had done just that on the parsley. I suspected that this baby was asleep and began its own adventure from NC to FL in the cargo space of my SUV.

Along with the potted plants were bags of purchases, my luggage, and my soft leather briefcase. Because he was in the hallway between my office, where I had dropped my briefcase, and my bedroom, I suspected that he had slipped into my briefcase, which I rarely zipped shut, to feel safe.

No, I was not happy that he was in my house, but the alternatives were more unsettling. What if he slithered under the car seats to join me as a passenger? That could have been an ugly, and perhaps dangerous scene. I can't imagine the chaos that could have erupted on the highway. Or worse yet, what if he were still in my briefcase when I reached in to find something? Let that sink in.

Why do I think God was having some fun? Because of the possibilities for disastrous events and revolting events were so many and because none of them happened. Except in my mind, of course, where all of those possibilities loomed large. Consider first the possibility that the little guy had slithered its way to the floorboard between my feet or next to me in the passenger footwell. Surprises such as that are not good, traveling at 70 miles per hour on the freeway. I don't know how calm I could have remained.

Or consider the heart-stopping possibility that I had not noticed the baby's colorful movement and it had made the trip into my bedroom. Talk about a living nightmare of possibilities! I'll let you create your own fantasy here. The scenarios abound. None of them are particularly good.

Or equally as heart-stopping is the possibility that the baby had been too scared to leave the cozy confines of my briefcase, and I reached in for a pen, or my small stapler, or a marker. Grabbing a hold of the baby as I searched for something, or even peering in to look for what I needed and finding the baby, instead! God just let my inventive mind master the possibilities of all the "could've been's." He's probably laughing again, now.

I suspect that God is a fairly serious sort of super deity, except when he isn't.

God's Creativity

Only God can paint
a sky full of pictures with stars
for the eye to see.

And he stirs the seas
from their calmness to fierceness
in His artist's zeal.

Each sparrow flies free,
every bee finds its own blooms
and God takes pleasure.

He watches the leaves
shimmer and dance on their stems,
each part of the whole.

Nothing escape's God's
plan for a joyful world view
of his handiwork.

Drive Through It! Drive Through It!

This vignette came to me as the picture of an old car popping onto the freeway at a place of unauthorized entry. The car plopped down and blocked both lanes. The voice told me "I was with you." The voice also had told me to "Drive Through It!"

My friend and I were on our way to Shenandoah National Park in Virginia. Specifically, we would be staying in cabins once used by the Civil Conservation Core (CCC) workers when the men were building shelters in and other enhancements to our national park system, including its roadways. We planned to spend time living in her family history. Her dad had worked in the CCC to help support his family. She couldn't recall in which state he had worked, but spending some time in a CCC camp was close enough.

We would be staying in an original wood frame CCC cabin. The brochure said it had been "modernized" with air-conditioning. The big thing was room rent was, as I recall, about $50 a day.

The night before, we had enjoyed a summer rainfall in the shelter of a huge pole barn, immersed in wonderful bluegrass music, in Charlottesville, VA. The event was billed as a fiddler's convention, but there were a whole lot more banjos, string basses, and guitars than fiddles. It didn't matter. The music was magic from another place and time in our lives. When we left Charlottesville in the morning, we cut across the countryside to U.S. 64 on our way north to Big Meadow, part of the U.S. park service.

The day was perfect for traveling. The roadway was clear, well-maintained, pleasant to drive. An 18-wheeler and I rolled along at 55, the speed limit. No traffic lay ahead. Traffic behind us was still tiny dots on the horizon.

We drove along nicely, the trucker and I, for maybe 30 miles on the open road. When the truck labored uphill, I lazily passed it. On its downhill run, the truck surged past me. We did this vehicle do-si-do with aplomb. The knot of trailing traffic was gaining on us. The speed merchants, for whom a speed limit clearly matters not, would catch up sooner, rather than later.

PREVENIENT GRACE

The trucker and I traveled in this easy rhythm for a few miles more. Our ease was rudely impeded when we rolled over the top of the next hill, however.

Less than the length of a football field ahead, an aged car, a maroon-colored boat of a vehicle had illegally crossed the median and entered the highway at an unauthorized entry point. The driver accelerated to get onto the two-lane highway in this unofficial entry, his entry faltered. His vehicle leaped over the rough edge of the highway and skewed in his landing. I had begun to break, the trucker was doing the same, but the car sat crosswise of the roadway, mostly in my lane. The 18-wheeler was full on my right. Thoughts of how to survive this challenge raced through my mind. I knew the speeding vehicles would soon be breaking over the hill behind us and slamming on the brakes could make this bad situation worse. Before I could think another thought, a strong, persistent-but-calm voice repeated, "Drive through it! Drive through it!" Drive through it I did.

I have no idea what my speed was when I drove onto the shoulder and to the left of the fool in the clunker sitting in my lane, but I kept it as even as I could. I had never been in a critical traffic situation before. This was a very new and very scary incident.

As soon as my car hit that washboard of speed bumps, my eyeballs crossed and danced in their sockets. My cheeks and jowls flopped on my facial skeleton. My hands and arms shook numbingly. Good grief! That washboard was devised to alert sleepy drivers when they strayed from the roadway, not for continuous travel for any length of time. But there I was driving straight ahead, hoping to avoid a huge crash.

At this point, I had no idea where the knucklehead driver was, but I hoped that he had stayed put and was not trying to return to the shoulder. As my body flopped and shook, I glimpsed a maroon blur through the passenger window. "Thank you, God!" I thought. We had cleared the danger. I bumped back onto the highway, regained my senses, and looked for the nearest exit.

I also checked my rearview mirror and quickly scanned for the fool in maroon. The mass of speed demons was well on their way down the hill, closing in on the truck and me. Given the way the traffic was moving, it appeared that those drivers were unaware of the drama in the minutes before. The maroon clunker sat on the right shoulder. I hoped terrible things for him. Things like: I hope you soiled your pants and were on your way to an important appointment. I hope your car won't start. I hope wherever you are going you will be late. Well, actually, I didn't really want those things for him, but I was experiencing the anger that comes with being threatened with terrible injury or death and the sense of relief that follows. If I had been in the same physical place as he, I might have charged at him with all the rage that I felt at that moment.

The command to "Drive through it!" had saved our lives. Drivers are not schooled in crisis management in highway driving, and I had not a clue of what to do in this situation. No driver gets a test run at highway crashes. What a memorable experience "Drive through it!" had become.

I checked my rearview mirror again and saw that the fool and his vehicle were still sitting on the right shoulder. Probably needed a change of clothes.

Speaking of "our lives," my traveling companion had been asleep when the ordeal began. In the middle of the shaking and rattling, she sat upright and hollered, "What the hell, Foor?" I hadn't taken time to wake her when the crisis began. I was way too busy. Besides that, if we were going to die, she might as well be asleep when it happened, rather than scream her way to eternity. "Not now!" I hollered back. I was trying to stay composed until I got off the freeway.

At the exit, I paced and stalked and paced, my fists balled, my body stiff, tense at the rear of the parking lot. Guttural sounds began to roll in my throat until they finally rose to a massive roar toward the sky. I was alive. My friend and I still were able to visit the CCC camp in Big Meadow. Our families would not have to collect pieces of us in pine boxes. As the voice had commanded, we had driven through it.

Glory to God at Cracker Barrel

The rain blows in sheets.
The diners jog hurriedly.
I rock joyfully on the porch.

In retirement I am free to play
In the fullness of your gifts
In which I daily revel joyfully.

I rock in rhythm to the music
from inside and smile at the
heated sizzle of the rain.

Life so abundant that my heart
Fills my soul with sweet moments.
I treasure your gifts and rock.

You gift me with grace
So full and rich it takes my breath.
I smile, and I rock.

Success after 57 Years

The vignette for this story came as I was writing about the scary revival meeting that I had attended when I was a kid of 12 years old. In the vignette, I was standing in front of the humanities building at State College of Florida, feeling buoyed about accomplishing what had been taken from me decades ago; my college degree. It was a sunny day on campus, made even sunnier by my decision to seek that elusive degree.

The receptionist at the Renaissance Center completed her transaction with the woman in line before me, and I moved toward the counter. The receptionist, whose attitude was as tightly wound as her hair, ignored me. She knew I was there. She had given me a disdainful, raised eyebrow look over the previous customer's shoulder.

PREVENIENT GRACE

I had come to the Renaissance Center, the community's official senior center in Bradenton, FL, ready to sign up as an official senior. Age wise, I am a senior. Nevertheless, I had not felt like a senior until I survived chemotherapy for breast cancer.

Weeks earlier, I had completed a year of chemotherapy to wipe out the cancer that resulted in my second mastectomy. The treatments had gone well, but now my brain was muddled. Simple tasks that had been routine a year ago challenged me.

This confusion frustrated me. To my way of thinking, I was seriously diminished. This possibility that I was mentally diminished angered me. To this point, my life had been energizing, interesting, enjoyable. What will become of me now?

"You are experiencing confusion from your chemo treatments," my oncologist told me. He suggested I read new books, start a new hobby, make lists, and other suggestions common to overcoming brain diminishment in the elderly.

The "You are getting old. So, what?" kind of thinking for a brain that had served me so well for 68 years was unacceptable. Until chemotherapy, I could easily complete basic math computations in my head. At this point, however, I was unable to add a column of even simple numbers in my head. How frustrating and annoying.

"Lord, deliver me from being a mental vegetable for the rest of my life," I thought.

Thanks to the wonder of technology, I was able to easily research the possibility of a more satisfying solution to my brain drain. My research showed that with some "serious effort" I could improve my thought patterns, my ability to think objectively, and do it systematically, efficiently.

I must, according to the literature, challenge my brain to heal itself. The challenge would require more than solving *The New York Times* crossword puzzle and making reminder lists. Which is why I showed up at the Renaissance Center. The center's online literature said that Tai Chi was the most popular class among senior citizens. Perhaps memorizing the system of moves and concentrating to execute them gracefully would begin the healing process.

Th Renaissance Center clearly was not going to be an answer. The receptionist never acknowledged my presence in her space. I slapped the brochure onto the counter and walked out. "What now?" I wondered.

I walked to my car, muttering about her rudeness and lack of respect. Again, I wondered, "Now what?" I started driving, thinking of possible alternatives to the failed plan. None came to mind. My wandering delivered me to the front parking lot at State College of Florida. "What the heck? Why am I here?"

"Administration Building—Testing," the sign said, with an arrow pointing the way.

"Testing for college classes? Seriously? And then, "Why not?" I had nothing else to do with my life, my time is my own. I returned the next day, during regular testing hours, and completed a couple of hours of basic testing in math and English.

After 55 years out of school, I needed two remedial-math classes and English 101, which was required of all new students. If math, a difficult subject for me, didn't stir the regrowth of my synapses and dendrites, what topic might? English had been fun since my first class in elementary school. It was like a game with words. I completed the remedial college math and the mandatory English class. I was having fun, even in math, so I decided to keep on keepin' on. The next semester I took another math class, and classes in ethics and humanities. I earned A's in each of them. I was taking classes that interested me to facilitate brain growth and loving every minute of every class.

One day, as I walked cross the SCF campus, I realized that I was walking in the presence of opportunity and success. I smiled. The college degree that eluded me in 1956 was within my reach. I turned on my heel and headed for the counseling office. I wanted to know what I had to do to earn my AA degree.

If I worked diligently, the counselor said, I could acquire that prize in 2011. Because I had amassed enough transferable credits from years of classes at Black Hawk College in Illinois, I had fewer classes to complete. As a mother of four children, I had sought adult contact and mental stimulation, so I had taken many classes in art and psychology and sociology. Because my husband taught math in night classes, I was able to take credit courses for free.

Now, as I approached graduation from SCF, I asked the "Now what?" question of a friend at lunch one day. She suggested I enter the Program for Experienced Learners at Eckerd College in St. Petersburg, just across Tampa Bay. She had completed the PEL program and then earned her master's degree in Colorado. She said the PEL program was unique and daunting. She was spot on. PEL students could take no more than two courses per semester because each course met five-hours twice weekly, for eight weeks.

We "experienced learners" produced in eight weeks what the regular students, the young ones, did in 16. In my final semester, I had two literature classes. Two books a week, with interpretive essays expected for each of them. Yes, I read and wrote well into the nights. This snafu was an accident of class availability, not lack of planning. Nevertheless, when I submitted the final papers for that semester, I knew that I had climbed an academic mountain.

In reality, the whole college experience was daunting, yet exhilarating and joyful. I was the eldest in all of my classes—by about 25 years. This challenged me to rise above my stereotypical thinking—and theirs—about how "elders" should behave. I got over that nonsense soon enough. My advanced age changed the warp and the weft of the classes, and it pleased me that my experiences added valuable depth and texture to their learning. Moreover, the younger students introduced me to the finer points of "now," awareness of current thinking and attitudes.

On both graduation days, my family—five children, spouses or significant others, and my granddaughter—cheered and hooted loudly as I proudly walked across the stage and accepted my diploma from the president of each college.

My pride in accomplishment and satisfaction were doubled when I reminded myself that the journey toward a college degree that should have begun in 1956, when I was 18, ended 57 years later, at age 75.

SHIRLEY J FOOR

On May 12, 2013, I proudly held my BA in fine arts, magna cum laude, along with the college's coveted award for my writing portfolio.

Time and Tide and All that Jazz

This not a story about prevenient grace. I thought that you should know the rest of the grace story: The gifts of grace do not stop; the grace that just gets better when you know that you are walking with God. When you allow yourself to be in tune with God, when you embrace the notion that God can and does speak to you at any time and in many ways, your life becomes richer. Prevenient grace brings you to the important gift of daily grace.

The gift of grace is awesome. The gift of grace I write about in this story brought such a magnificent moment of discovery to my life that I am compelled to share it.

To have your own moments like this one, you need two things: one is to believe that God wants you to enjoy life in every way, with small and large moments of joyful discovery, and two, to pay attention to and to acknowledge the seemingly random "aha!"

sensations when you know in your heart and soul that something unusual is taking place, or is about to take place, in your presence. And now, my exceptional "aha" experience.

We who live close to oceans and rivers that flow into oceans notice the tide activity. It goes out, and it comes in. The tide goes out, and we have a beach; the tide returns, and we'll visit the beach another day. The comings and the goings of the tide are very predictable and predicted with care for things such as fishing, boating, and shipping. The results of the ebb and the flow appear on the water-marked walls in canals. But have you ever seen the tide hover between its coming and its going? I have, and the sight was a gift of extraordinary pleasure and absolute wonder.

My daughters, Laurie and Sharon, and I had driven to Savannah for a girls' weekend. At that moment in time, we were enjoying the lunch on the Savannah River paddle wheeler. The buffet was great, the afternoon mild, and the gliding shoreline mesmerizing.

After lunch, we took our drinks outside to the deck chairs. Before long, a gaggle of women rearranged the deck chairs next to me and were chattering, giggling heartily. A little beyond them, toward the bow, hung the speaker that was carrying the muffled, muddled voice of the boat's narrator. (Every ride has a narrator these days.) I didn't care enough about the narrator's story to strain my ears, I sipped my iced tea and let my thoughts drift with the boat.

Then, above the cacophony, came these clear words: world's largest cargo ship, tonight, low tide, between 6 and 7 p.m. Other very muffled words were mixed in with those, but I received the message: Something unusual was coming my way tonight.

It was mid-afternoon when our luncheon cruise returned to the dock. Out of deference to their aging mother, the girls suggested that we return to our rooms and rest before dinner. Sharon and I were sharing a room, Laurie was a few doors away. While I napped, Sharon read. When I awoke, I was thinking about the "world's largest cargo ship." So was Sharon.

"I really would like to see that cargo ship," she said, with shy interest. Her tone of voice was asking, "How about you?"

"Me, too. Let's do it!" As I slipped into my shoes, splashed some water on my face, and combed my hair, Sharon called her sister to invite her along. Laurie declined our invitation, however. Our dinner could wait until after the waterfront excursion.

It was then 5 o'clock, and our hotel was about a six-block walk to a concrete bench on the river walk. Due to the deliberate and determined gait of this old girl, we arrived at the walkway by the river by about 5:45. We watched the interesting collection of people stroll by our bench and peered down toward the port. While we peered, we also swatted no-see-ums, the population of which seemed to grow by the minute. Those tiny creatures have the smallest mouths and the biggest darned bites ever. We were not deterred, however. We wanted to see the monster cargo ship.

We swatted and itched for about an hour because the ship departed closer to 7 p.m. "Here it comes," Sharon said, as she reached over and grabbed my arm. "I think that's it, anyway." In the distance, still among the distant buildings and docks, a massive shape, big, black, foreboding, seemed to squeeze around the turn from the big loading docks toward the bridge that arched over the Savannah River.

While Sharon had been watching for the freighter, my attention had been drawn to the river. I realized that the river had changed. All day, the Savannah River had been churning along at 15 to 20 miles an hour, maybe faster, toward the Atlantic Ocean. Now, the choppiness had smoothed, the current was dramatically slower than when we first arrived at riverside 30 minutes ago. The current had slowed still more since we had taken our seats. Now, the water was barely moving. Little eddies formed, swirled and dissipated in the splotches of reflected light in the center of the river.

As I watched, I had an "aha!" moment. I realized how carefully science and nature were working together to make sure that the massive ship approaching the bridge would arrive at low tide, not a minute before, so that the behemoth could glide safely under the steel arch on its way to the ocean.

My vigil vacillated between the approaching ship and the continual change in the river's speed and attitude. The incredible silhouette loomed larger as it approached the bridge, and the river calmed still more.

The river lingered between its coming and its going. It was like God was saying, "Pay attention to this. I want you to see my power." The massive blackness drew closer to the bridge and the traffic rolling over it. Then Lady Savannah seemed to throw back her watery skirts in a respectful curtesy. She drew the water toward the ocean behind her just a little bit more and waited while the freighter slid safely under the bridge. Although I was unable to see it because the freighter was so massive, I believe the outgoing current became the incoming current, as the ship traveled the half mile or so to the ocean. How absolutely extraordinary to witness the moment when the river suspended its flow between its coming and its going.

Although the impending darkness shrouded the view of the freighter gliding under the bridge and the steady flow of traffic, I strained to see that moment. Ships have no brakes, so the decision makers needed to be right on the money in their calculations about the tide and the time it would take to travel from the loading dock to the bridge. Even if there were a mistake and the captain immediately reversed the freighter's mighty engines to avoid a collision, the momentum of the ship's weight and the lack of resistance on the river would carry the ship forward for a mile, maybe more, before it could stop. If the captain and the pilot had miscalculated the time and the tide, the bridge would be a "goner," like Florida's Sunshine Skyway in 1982, and become a pile of twisted rubble in the shipping channel of the world's eighth largest seaport.

How big was this ship? Breathtakingly big, but its hugeness is difficult to explain. The comparison that comes to mind is a local one, the Home Depot on Cortez Road in Bradenton FL. The Home Depots do seem to be constructed very similarly, so maybe the comparison will take shape.

The ship was roughly as wide as half of the Home Depot's length. The ship was as long as, if not longer than, the Home Depot, from its commercial department on one end to its garden shop on the other.

And the height? Well, that was something else. The ship above water was at least Home Depot high, with another Home-Depot height of containerized cargo piled atop its deck. Its size was especially imposing in the darkness and the comparative narrowness of the Savannah River.

The freighter passed by the River Walk with barely a sound. The freighter's size was so overwhelming and dark that no one on the walkway seemed to even notice the historic event taking place next to them.

Night had encroached upon the scene, as I watched the exceptional dance between science and nature move and hover at just the right times, keeping life on the river safe and productive. What an extraordinary, definitely a one-of-a-kind, experience had been granted to me that night.

•. •. •. • •

Now about the gift of grace. First, God sent the details about the freighter clearly through the muddled sound from the speaker. Its clarity so pierced the distracting noises that I could not miss it. I knew that the message was for me. I have grown accustomed to these kinds of messages.

Then, as I watched for the freighter, the reason Sharon and I were *determinedly braving the no-see-ums, He turned my attention to the reason that **I** was in that place at that particular time. He wanted me to bear witness and to gift me with this singular vision of the wonder of His power. Yes, yes, I know about the moon's gravitational pull and that the tides are a natural result of that pull. I believe, however, that our Creator put together all of the pieces of the 3D puzzle called our world. Newton might have named the gravitational, but God put the words into his mouth and the understanding into Newton's brain.*

Coincidences do not exist.

These days, watching the tide come and go at the beach or the shore is pretty ordinary when compared to the way more impressive moment when the tide hovers between that coming and going.

Refuge in the Light

You stir the oceans
Until the fiercest of waves
Build upon one another.

Their power and foam
Crash down on the small lighthouse
Hiding its strong light.

The turmoil pulls back
And gathers strength once again.
The eye of light shines.

You are that light, Lord.
As the turmoil pounds us,
Your strong light breaks through.

Epilogue

Well, we are at the end of my stories of prevenient grace.

Perhaps you are muttering that I have persuaded you of nothing new about this prevenient grace thing or your relationship with God. You may even have dismissed your own possibilities of grace with a Bah Humbug! That's okay. I know that I am not the only person God chose to take notice of His persistent gifts of prevenient grace. Nevertheless, I believe God charged me with telling my story so that prevenient grace would live in more than scholarly words; it would have a voice. Persuading you that He has gifted you with prevenient grace over your lifetimes is His job, not mine. Obviously, my words drew you through the open door to a moment of thoughtful exploration. What you do with this opportunity also is between you and God.

PREVENIENT GRACE

Oh, no, you don't get to turn away. You have taken the step. Looking away may save you from commitment for a time, but now you know something of prevenient grace, and God knows that you know. It is possible that I may have written sentence upon sentence of these difficult remembrances just for you. Or maybe not. I know only that God directed me and insisted that I commit these stories to paper.

Following His path, this particular path of personal disclosure, has been draining.

When I flagged on my follow-through or withheld a scintilla of truth or of authenticity to protect myself from your criticism, He put obstacles in my pathway to prevent me from completing plans for other writing projects. God has this rule, much like the rule of any parent who wants his child to grow in righteousness: I have given you a specific task. Until you finish it and finish it to my standards, you will not reach the top of your mountain. I shall keep you circling and circling around your mountain until you get the message. Just do it!

Well, I circled the mountain a couple of times, maybe more, before I heard His admonition: "I am waiting for your honest words."

Telling the truth and nothing but the truth about serious, personal, unspoken events in my life has been a mountain unto itself. So, you see, just as I fretted about your expectations in learning about the "God connection," I also held back, at times, because I expected that you would judge the validity of my stories of the gifts of prevenient grace. The fullness of the revelations, as God had admonished me to share, would surely test your patience. Needless to say, I expected that your stern criticism, your condemnation, and your disbelief would spill into my life like indelible blue ink on a blotter; forever a stain on my sense of reason.

At times, God took stern issue that I even thought that your disapproval should matter. God is loving, but He also can be downright prickly when you don't cross His "Ts" and dot His "Is." This is especially true when one fails to be authentic. So, I stopped caring about you and kept writing the truth of my experiences, as best as I could recall them, with the Lord's help.

It was those times that gave me heartburn. You might still think that I wrote these stories to soothe my ego, or to put a personal pity party into print. If you think I soothed some egocentric bent, I assure you that it was not pleasant to publicly relive nearly 30 hours of labor or the 43 days of hospitalization in dire peril for my life, or seeing my beautiful daughter with fatty tumors all over her body. No, I relinquished my privacy and my sensibilities because God asked me to write the painful truth for you. Maybe just for you. Maybe I am the conduit to help you understand how He also has influenced your life, even when you were not yet in touch with Him.

However, I did not write about everything. For instance, I did not write about the times that God spoke through me to someone else. I thought that those stories surely would stretch your patience. Still, in my heart, I believe that God has blessed you a time or two with being His voice, His messenger. You know, the times you spoke words that were a surprise to you, but the person to whom you spoke them behaved as though you were the wisest person ever. Ah, I perceive a moment of recognition of that awareness on your face right now.

I am no more important or special than you. Each of us is valuable in God's sight, but some of us have been a bit slow in recognizing His voice, His call to us.

Prevenient grace has been at work in your life. The trail of spiritual breadcrumbs is as varied and as surprising as the Lord is constant, trustworthy, and faithful, but the trail is there. Soon enough, you will accept His message. When you do, say a prayer for me.

One last point. Look away from the "good Christians" who would, by their knowledge of scriptures and their many imposing thou shalts or thou shalt nots of the Old Testament, seek to dissuade you from believing in your heart, mind, and soul that you are as grand in God's sight as they. If you listen carefully, the still, small voice of God will wash over their drone of pomposity that is meant to impress and to intimidate you. That distracting noise also is the devil working through their deceptive piety to keep a hold on you to confuse you.

If the words in this book, my disclosures of prevenient grace, have drawn you into your time of discovery, then praise Him. You, my friend, have come of age in the time of the New Testament. This is the time not of laws but of the time to be joyful in your walk with the Lord. Measure your steps with Jesus' in love and joyful freedom in that walk. Yes, you still must be mindful of your innate nature to sin, because you surely will sin, but say that you are sorry, ask forgiveness, and keep walking in joy.

About the Author

Shirley Foor began writing in the free-lance market more than 50 years ago. Free-lance writing allowed her to earn a little money while she stayed home with her four children.

Then Shirley's husband broke his back, and Shirley became the breadwinner. Her background in free-lance writing gave her entry to a job as a features writer at the local newspaper in Moline, Il. Over the years, she was a reporter, chief of three bureau offices, and assistant regional editor.

When she was denied promotion to the Regional Editor's position because she was "unqualified," she left Illinois for a City Editor's job at a Knight-Ridder newspaper in Bradenton, Florida, She was the first female city editor and later became the first female managing editor at that newspaper.

SHIRLEY J FOOR

Shirley left journalism after 20 years and continued to write about her experiences and observations for family and friends, breaking from the "facts only" regimen of journalism to pursue the freedom and the joy of creative nonfiction storytelling. The facts are there, so is the context of the moment and the experience. Her first book, *Confound It!: A Collection of Recollections* is a gathering of stories from the archives of Stories Foortold.

Confound It!: A Collection of Recollections is available from Amazon.com at this link:
https://www.amazon.com/Confound-Collection-Recollections-Shirley-Foor/dp/195049909X

www.ingramcontent.com/pod-product-compliance
Lightning Source LLC
Chambersburg PA
CBHW022117040426
42450CB00006B/733